From Survivor to Surgeon

From Survivor to Surgeon:
A Refugee's Memoir of Perseverance and Purpose

Book and cover design by Kevin Breen

ISBN: 978-1-957607-10-8
Cataloging-in-Publication Data is available upon request

Manufactured in the United States of America

Published by Latah Books
www.latahbooks.com

Latah Books and the author are grateful to Spokane Arts for
its generous support of this project.

FROM SURVIVOR TO SURGEON

A Refugee's Memoir
of Perseverance and Purpose

By Paul Luu, MD
with Christopher Maccini

Dedication

Dedicated to all those who helped me along my journey:

My parents and siblings.

My high school teachers: Mr. Frank Wilgus, Mrs. Silvia Moran, Mrs. Judy Chilcott, and Mr. Raymond Chayo.

My professors and mentors at University of the Pacific: Paul A. Richmond, Ph.D., Ernst Belz, Foad Nahai, Ph.D., and Mrs. Sidney Hickey.

My mentor at UCLA School of Medicine: Dr. Malcolm A. Lesavoy.

My foster family: Mr. and Mrs. Lyle and Lena Baumann, and Linda Graham.

And my mentor at Tulane University: Dr. Samuel Perry.

Thank you all.

Contents

Preface

Many stories have been told about the civil war that ripped the country of my birth in two, about the millions of lives lost and devastated in what has become known in the United States as the Vietnam War, but which the Vietnamese refer to as the Resistance War Against America. That conflict, along with the political upheaval and bloody war with the Khmer Rouge in Cambodia that followed, created the largest refugee crisis since World War II. More than three million Vietnamese, Cambodian, Hmong, and Laotian people fled their homes. Hundreds of thousands escaped by boat across dangerous, pirate-patrolled seas. Many did not survive.

At the age of sixteen, I became one of these "boat people."

But this is not a story of war. That period of death, destruction, and radical change is something from which many of my countrymen never recovered. Yet, in the midst of tragedy, the true resilience of the human spirit is revealed. Even amid such horror, lives can be transformed. Individuals can be reborn.

I began my journey as a refugee, a survivor. I became a foster child and diligent student. I faced countless challenges but was also given boundless opportunities. A new country offered me refuge. Teachers and mentors and friends gave me guidance. I saw kindness I could never repay. Through hard work, perseverance, and more than a bit of luck, I became a doctor—a surgeon—and I forged a new life for myself that I could have never imagined as a child growing up in a country at war.

This is my story, and it is my hope that readers will see in it the value of all people, especially those forced to leave their homes because of war. I hope my story will remind those who are fortunate to open their arms and hearts to those who have less, who are striving for the American Dream. By sharing my experience, I hope I can inspire others to overcome their own challenges, whatever they may be.

NOTE: Some names have been changed to protect individuals' privacy.

1. A Childhood at War

On April 30th, 1975, the Communist North Vietnamese Army entered the city of Saigon, rolling through the streets in tanks and armored transports. For two days, the ground shook like an earthquake from the war machines rumbling past my house. I overheard my parents and other adults saying, *Things are going to be different now. Things are going to be more difficult.* Meanwhile, the tanks crashed through the gates of Independence Palace, where Dương Văn Minh, president of South Vietnam, surrendered and formally dissolved the government of South Vietnam. The war was over. The country was unified under communist control. I was twelve years old.

Strange as it may sound, before that day, the war affected me very little. In many ways I had a normal Vietnamese childhood, even while the country was engulfed in war. My parents had moved to Saigon from northern Vietnam in 1954 when the country was first divided. They believed then that they had escaped communist rule, and they opened a small store in a neighborhood market called Chợ Vườn Chuối, which translates literally as "banana farm market." In a one-room flat above the store lived our entire family: my mother and father, my five sisters, my older brother, Tài, and me, Tiến Kim Lưu. Only once, during the Tet Offensive of 1968, do I remember the sound of bombers in the sky and the worry on my parents' faces. We had to go to another part of Saigon to stay with my uncle until the fighting receded.

Our flat above the store consisted of a single main room, about 450 square feet, where all nine of us slept on the floor, lined up like sardines in a tin. Looking back, I often wonder how my parents found the space intimate enough to create seven children. Once, I recall seeing them in the shower together, naked—a strange sight that I did not understand, though it made me realize the bathroom could be a private place. Later on, when I knew a spanking was coming my way—as it so often was—I sometimes escaped and locked myself in the bathroom.

It was a lucky day in my childhood if I did not get spanked by my mother or my oldest sister. Lucky because growing up, I was constantly in motion—talking and playing—in a world my mother tried desperately to control. For my parents, making an honest living as shopkeepers and meeting the needs of their neighbors was enough. But my mother firmly believed that her children were meant for bigger and better things. She expected my siblings and me to graduate from high school, go to college—maybe even overseas in a Western country—and become engineers and lawyers. In order to achieve this, my mother sequestered us from what she called "distractions."

Really, that meant anything outside of school, chores, and study. So keen was my mother on executing her plan, so clear on the discipline required to achieve this level of success, that her siblings began sending their children to our house, hoping they might flourish under her rigor.

Ironically, the migration of my cousins from down the street resulted in a windfall for me. While my imagination could satisfy me for long hours at a time, I always longed for more playmates. And I needed them to come to me because stepping outside the perimeter of our store was off limits. My brother, Tài, only a few years older than me, could have been a playmate. But he was a stereotypical Vietnamese boy, solemn and serious. To me, he was boring. I wanted to play. And so, I played with the girls: my sisters and a steady flow of female cousins sent by their parents hoping for a more academic, controlled environment—one I was intent on disrupting.

Every morning, I waited for the competition to arrive and the games to begin. I had to be careful to remain calm and not upset my mother early in the day. An early miscalculation could lead to a spanking or worse: confinement and a day off from play. Frequently, the cause of my mischief was my overactive curiosity. As many children do, I wondered about the world around me, and my constant questions exasperated my mother to no end.

One of my earliest memories is of glimpsing the delicate fabric of my sister's underpants sticking out from her school skirt. Naturally, I asked her, "Mama, what is that?"

She responded in horror, "Never ask such an inappropriate question!" She swatted my backside and sent me away.

How was I supposed to know what was appropriate? I only wanted to learn more about the world. Maybe I should have learned to keep my questions to myself, but my curiosity always outweighed my fear of spankings. The questions continued to burst out of me before I had the chance to consider their appropriateness.

On the days when I was finally allowed to play, I became the game master. During these games, I learned my first lessons in self-confidence and skill. Because I was a small boy, hyperactive and with a high-pitched voice, other boys often teased me. I could never keep up in athletic pursuits. But playing in small spaces—only a few square meters in the store or a corner of the outdoor market—called for games of quickness and coordination rather than physical prowess. The moving objects were small, the motion constricted, the player's success all dependent on hand-eye coordination— something I realized I possessed.

The games we played were simple, invented with what we had. We jumped rope and played a version of "pick up sticks" with chopsticks and a tennis ball. For hours every day, I played games with my sisters and cousins. I almost always won, and I began to understand the thrill of competition. I wanted to be the best. If somehow one of the girls beat me at a game, I became quiet and withdrawn, angry at myself for my weakness. I would sulk and replay the game over and over, considering my missteps and ensuring that I would never make them again. In the next game, I forged ahead with renewed intensity and a deeper desire to win.

I can't say for sure that these early games of coordination

and dexterity influenced my decision many years later to become a surgeon, but I know they had an impact on my penchant for competition. Excluded from the masculine world of physical sports, I relished these "girls' games" as an outlet for my energy and curiosity. Early in life, I learned to rely on my intelligence and skill in order to get ahead. Later, these same attributes would allow me to survive and overcome the many challenges that lay before me.

***

After the communists arrived in 1975, things began to change quickly. By that time, my parents' store had been doing well enough that they'd been able to buy the store adjacent to theirs. Later, they sold the combined, larger store and raised enough money to move our family across town. They purchased a store in the Truong Minh Giang market, a more central location off one of Saigon's main streets. We moved into a slightly larger apartment above the store. It was a modest change, but when you're used to sleeping in a small room with your entire family, even a bit more space feels like an enormous upgrade!

Despite the war, my parents did their best to improve their situation and provide the best life for our family. They began paying tuition for me, my brother, and my second oldest sister to attend a private French Catholic school. The school was near the famous old cathedral in the center of Saigon. My parents hoped that the Catholic school's discipline and superior education would lead us to a more prosperous future.

Perhaps we might even learn enough of the language to attend college in France or another Western country.

In school, I found that my competitive nature served me well, especially in math. My favorite subject was geometry. It reminded me of the games I'd played in the store—figuring out angles, solving problems. I always wanted to be first to solve any question the teacher asked, to be the top of the class—particularly in science and math.

During our free time at school, I played foosball with the other boys. I could never compete on a real soccer field, but foosball was something I excelled at. The game required quickness and coordination, as well as an intuitive understanding of geometry and angles. Of the one hundred or so children at the school, I was in the top six. There was a special foosball table reserved for the best players, and we placed bets of a dime or a nickel per game—serious money for a kid in Vietnam! Often, I found myself playing against one boy, a small, quiet student named Khoa. Like me, he was hard-working and intelligent. He had a quick shot that sometimes surprised me, sneaking through for a goal. But I usually managed to come back and win the game.

Sometimes, we played doubles, and my partner was a boy named Hoang. He was a decent player, but he wasn't quite as quick as I was. I admittedly looked down on him because he was also slower than me in the classroom. Other boys were smart, but I was smarter. Other boys were quick, but I was quicker. I was the best, and I knew it.

And then the communists took over Saigon. At the time, I was in the sixth grade. The communists distrusted foreign influence, especially from a Western country like France, and they threatened to shut down private schools like ours. For another year, I was able to attend the French school, but eventually, the new regime made good on their threats and closed the school. After that, all children had to attend their neighborhood school.

Consequently, I was sent to the local junior high school where I did my best to excel in the classroom. Quickly, I learned that there was a group of five boys who were considered the smartest in the class. I knew that I had to befriend them, to become part of their group. But this was not easy. Initially, they had no interest in welcoming me into their group. Part of their devotion to school came from the fact that all five boys were devout Catholics and they aspired to become priests. My family, on the other hand, were Buddhists. To these boys, I was a threat to their beliefs and a distraction from their academic and career goals.

I knew, even at that young age, that my intelligence was my greatest asset. I would never be accepted unless I could rise to the top of the class the way I had at my previous school. And so, I pursued these boys. I sat near them in class and followed them during our breaks. I even started hanging out at the Catholic church with them. We played badminton, where I held my own only because the game required great hand-eye coordination.

At the same time, I put all my efforts into beating these boys academically. I could hang around and pester them all I wanted, but if I couldn't show them that I was their intellectual peer, they would never accept me. And so, with hard work, that is what I did. I studied. When we took tests and had assignments in school, I began to beat even these smartest boys. And they took notice. Eventually, our time together became less strained. They opened up to me and began to talk about themselves, their lives. We became friends and soon, best friends.

After junior high, I moved to a communist-controlled high school. Before the communists reorganized the schools, Gia Long had been one of two famous all-girl schools in Saigon. The communists made it co-ed, but when I arrived in 1976, it was still 95 percent girls. I was one of only a handful of boys. You would think that this would have made my transition to the new school easier. I was used to playing with my sisters and female cousins. But it was not easy. Even though the boys were few, they still teased me for my small size and my high-pitched voice. All the girls had beautiful handwriting and decorations on their writing assignments. My handwriting was sloppy and embarrassing. I felt like an outcast among both genders.

While things changed for me at school, they also changed at home. Initially, my father supported the communists and their reunification efforts. The end of the war meant that my mother and father could now reconnect with many of their family members from the North whom they had not seen for over twenty years, since 1954 when the country became divided. Many of our family members came to Saigon after the war, and my father enjoyed playing the role of host. At home, he never allowed anything negative to be said about the new regime. No complaints about changing schools. No complaints about the requirement to hang the North

Vietnamese flag alongside a portrait of Ho Chi Minh inside our home. Any kind of behavior that involved "acting like Americans" was prohibited.

Whenever these poorer family members from the North visited, my parents felt obligated to give them money and gifts despite our already strained budget. Once, my mother said something negative about the communists and complained about my father's relatives. My father got angry at my mother's comments, and he hit her. It was one of the only times I remember my father being violent toward my mother. I knew things were changing, both within our family and throughout the country. We had entered a new and different world.

My father kept up his support for the communists even when they changed the country's currency, devaluing much of our savings. It wasn't until the government seized control of all private businesses—including my family's store—that my father finally began to hate the communists.

It was early in 1978, less than three years after the communists first arrived, that my family's store was taken over. Their whole adult lives, my parents had worked to establish that store. It was small, but it brought in enough money for our family to live on, and my parents were proud of it. It was the only thing they had.

One day, three soldiers wearing civilian clothes arrived at the market. They entered our store and, as calmly as if they were issuing a traffic ticket, ended the only livelihood my family knew. After ordering everyone to leave the store, one soldier stood in front of the door and read from an official letter. Our store had become the property of the state, he said. Private businesses like my parents' store were vestiges of imperialism and capitalism and would not be tolerated. While he read, the other two soldiers closed the door and locked the metal gate.

"Under no circumstances," the lead soldier said, glaring at our huddled family, "is anyone to enter the premises."

And just like that, the last remnant of my family's old life disappeared.

***

When the communist government took control of the market, we were forced to leave our small house above the store. This changed everything for me. Suddenly, my family's sole means of supporting itself was gone. We were told to relocate to the "new economic zone," a piece of jungle on the outskirts of Saigon. But my family knew it would be difficult to survive outside the familiarity of the city. Instead, my parents bribed a local official to ignore our presence. We couldn't stay in our home, but we were able to move across the city to stay with my uncle, my mother's cousin, and his family.

We became desperately poor, and my parents struggled to provide even the most basic necessities. Although all private enterprises were forbidden by the communist government, my parents set up an outdoor stand where they sold cold drinks. It was a far cry from our family store, but my parents had a good business sense and always did what they had to in order to provide for my siblings and me. Our cold drinks sold well, and my parents were able to start saving some money, buying gold in order to avoid the volatility of currency changes.

It was during this time that I learned one of the most important lessons of my life. After the government seized my family's store, we were forbidden from entering it to recover any of the valuable merchandise left behind. Soldiers patrolled the area to keep anyone from going in or out. But by waiting until late at night, we were able to get into the store and smuggle out a few items.

One item was a nice piece of wool fabric large enough to fashion into a pair of pants. To us, this was a rare and valuable thing. To keep it safe, I put the fabric in my backpack and brought it with me to school. I called upon my friends to help. Of the five boys I had befriended at school, there was one named Tran Quang Ai with whom I was particularly close.

Ai's family was from Huế, a city in central Vietnam that served as the country's capital prior to 1945. He spoke with a distinct accent, and because of that stood out from the other boys. He was also not an athlete. He didn't play badminton with the rest of us. But he was a simple, kind-hearted boy, and I knew he was trustworthy.

I asked him to hide the fabric for me. He knew—we both knew—that if he agreed, he would be putting his own family's safety in danger. If he was caught, he could be punished, jailed, maybe even killed. But he agreed.

At any point, he could have stolen the fabric and sold it himself. His family was as desperate as mine. But he held onto it, hiding it for me until I was able to collect it. Eventually, I was able to sell the fabric on the black market and bring in some money for my family.

Tran Quang Ai was a true friend. He taught me how valuable it is to have someone you can truly trust in a time of danger and need. It is a lesson I have never forgotten, and one I have tried to pass on to others in need.

***

Because my family was struggling so badly to get by, my brothers, sisters, and I all had to help. For me that usually meant working at the drink stand. In the morning, I woke up and went to school, and in the afternoons, I helped run the stand. My siblings and I would switch off, even days and odd days, working at the drink stand with our parents. Often, I would sleep at the stand, in constant fear of being awakened by police who could arrest me for being there. I would wake early the next morning and begin the cycle again. Suddenly, academics no longer seemed like a priority. The priority was survival. My grades began to slip.

My parents, who had always prioritized their children's studies above all else, were now too busy, too concerned about their finances to notice. And a funny thing happened. I realized that I no longer cared about school. After all those years of rigorous study and trying to be at the top of the class, I felt an enormous sense of relief. A new priority emerged. My whole life, I had been teased for being small, for being un-athletic. There I was, a teenager, still as puny as ever. With academics no longer on my mind, I decided to focus on exercising and getting strong.

Of course, this was a priority for the communist government as well. The country had just emerged from a decades-long war which had cost hundreds of thousands of lives, and already a new conflict was brewing along the border with Cambodia. A new war seemed imminent, and the government would need a fresh crop of strong young soldiers. All students were encouraged to exercise and join after-school sports teams.

All my life I had been a small, weak boy. I excelled at games that required quickness and cunning, but in athletic pursuits, I was hopeless. I remember hearing a rumor at that time that swimming made people taller. If you worked hard and became a strong swimmer, then you would grow into a bigger, stronger person. It seemed far-fetched, but I was willing to try anything. With the same determination I had always applied to school, I decided to become the next great swimming sensation. I went to sign up for the swim team, only to find that the roster was completely full. The only options left were track and field and ping pong. Given my history with games of hand-eye coordination, ping pong should have been a natural choice. I thought back on my days of dominating the foosball table at the French school. Ping pong would not be much different. But I was determined to become a "real athlete," someone who excelled at more than just parlor games. So I wrote my name on the list for track and field.

I was so excited. This was my first experience on a real sports team. On my days off from the drink stand, I started attending track practice. But of course, I was humiliated. Compared to the other boys, I was so small and skinny. What made me think that a sports team would be a place to escape ridicule? Every day, the other boys called me names. They told me to go practice with the girls. I became furious. I got upset with myself for being so small and weak. But I stuck with it.

Soon, track and field became the only thing I looked forward to. I was never a star, but it gave me a chance to get out of the house, away from the worry and expectations of my parents. Even on days when I couldn't practice, when I had to help with the drink stand, I found myself thinking about running. And I did get stronger. A little at a time, my body responded by building muscles and endurance. There was no way I could have known it then, but this small amount of strength and stamina would soon save my life.

The one thing track and field did not help was my grades. They had already started to slip, but now they were abysmal. I never studied or did homework. Every spare moment, I was either working or running. This was not good, because I was nearing the end of high school. At that time in Vietnam, students were required to take a final test to earn a high school diploma. Your score on the test determined whether or not you would be allowed to attend college. Meanwhile, war was brewing with Cambodia. The communist government had begun drafting young men into the military. The options for me were college or war.

At the time, half of all young men drafted were killed in battle. Joining the military felt like a death sentence. Yet, because my family had been labeled as capitalists for owning a private business, they were forever blacklisted by the communist government. Even if I did somehow score high enough on the exam, I would never be allowed to attend college. Faced with two impossible options, my parents decided on a third. They had to send me away. I had to escape Vietnam.

2. Saigon to Sea

Early on the afternoon of November 14, 1978, I returned home from school to find my mother waiting for me with a worried look on her face. She looked me in the eyes and said simply, "It is time for you to leave."

I was sixteen years old. I knew what she meant. Our family was not in a sustainable position. The conflict with Cambodia was escalating, and young men were being conscripted to fight. If I had any chance of surviving the next few years, something had to change. I packed one small black duffel bag with the only belongings I could take with me on my uncertain journey: a few T-shirts, one pair of long pants, some boxer shorts, and a single aluminum can of dried meat along with a small amount of powdered milk—rations in case of dire emergency.

As I finished packing, I sensed with absolute certainty that I would never see my parents again after that day. But Vietnamese culture is unsentimental. There were no tears on my mother's cheeks and no words of wisdom and life advice from my father, who was not even home when I left. I simply said goodbye to my mother as if I were leaving for another day at school. Then, my oldest sister and I walked silently out of the house and climbed into a three-wheeled bicycle taxi.

***

The first stop on the journey away from my old life was the home of three women, all ethnically Chinese. They were each married, but two of their husbands had disappeared, missing in action during the war. My sister was friends with the second oldest of these women. This middle sister—whose husband was a nurse and still lived with the family—connected us with the owners of a boat in a port city on Vietnam's southern coast. For this service, my family had paid her five Mot Luong gold bars (187.5 grams) plus $200 USD which I was supposed to send upon my arrival in a new country. This was an enormous sum of money for my struggling family. But if she could safely smuggle me to the coast and onto a boat, I would have a chance to escape Vietnam. It felt like my only option for survival.

When my sister and I arrived that evening, I was shuffled inside the house and told to remain absolutely silent. After ensuring that I was safely hidden, my sister climbed back into the cycle rickshaw and returned home.

I remained at that house for a few days, waiting as quietly as possible, until we were told late one night that it was time to move. Outside, a small, motorized rickshaw was waiting for us. We drove through the dark city streets to the checkpoint at the city limits of Saigon. On the way, the sisters gave me a

Chinese name and told me only to use this name from that point on. In those days, the communist government did not allow the free movement of its citizens. We were not allowed to leave Saigon to go into the countryside, much less to leave the country for any reason. But because of the communist government's growing conflict with China, people of Chinese ethnicity living in Vietnam were allowed—even encouraged to some extent—to leave from the countryside or by boat. This was far from official policy, but there was an unspoken agreement that it would be better for everyone if ethnic Chinese people left Vietnam.

It was our hope that by traveling with a Chinese family under a Chinese name, I would make it through the communist militarized checkpoints along our route. But there was no guarantee. My heart pounded in my throat as we approached the checkpoint in Saigon. If we could successfully make it through this one and out of the city, I knew the rest of the journey would prove much easier.

Our driver slowed the rickshaw as we approached the checkpoint. A guard armed with a rifle was leaning against the building, smoking a cigarette. We came to a stop, and the guard spat the half-smoked cigarette into the dirt and crushed it with the heel of his boot. He approached the vehicle and peered into the windows. In the back, crammed among ten other people, I shrank into myself, trying to appear as small as possible.

"Names and identification," the soldier demanded.

The driver handed him a small stack of papers—my fake documents hidden among the Chinese family's—and we each gave our names. I had practiced the Chinese pronunciation of my false name, and I tried my best to make the awkward syllables sound natural coming out of my mouth.

The soldier flipped idly through the papers, not scrutinizing them too closely. I felt at any moment he would discover me, pull me out of the vehicle and drag me away. I would be thrown in prison, beaten, tortured, or worse. I could barely hear the soldier's questions through the thundering of my own heartbeat in my ears.

But after another moment of tension, the soldier returned the papers to the driver and waved us through the checkpoint. I breathed a sigh of relief as the checkpoint building receded into the dark behind us. We were through. I had made it out of Saigon. I was alive and on the next leg of my journey to freedom.

***

We drove through the night and into the morning, south along dirt roads through the green hills and flooded rice fields of the Vietnamese countryside. We crossed the Mekong River and continued south toward the coast. After eight or nine hours on the road, we finally arrived in Bạc Liêu, a small city on the southeastern coast of Vietnam. There, we stopped in front of a modest house where another Chinese family lived, the brother of the three sisters from Saigon. The brother was married, and they had a young daughter. Their house hardly had room for additional visitors, but once again I was ushered inside and told not to leave the house under any circumstances.

My stay there was illegal, and if discovered, the whole family would be in danger.

I thought I might be required to stay there for a few days, maybe a week at the most, but for some reason the boat's preparation was delayed. Each time we heard news, it was the same: the boat was not yet ready. Another delay. I began to think I might spend the rest of my life stuck in this small house among this Chinese family, doing my best to stay out of the way, trying to remain quiet, never stepping outside even to breathe the fresh, ocean-scented air.

I spent the whole season there, through Christmas and Chinese New Year, and into the following months. Finally, on March 10, 1979, word came that the boat was ready. The plan was to embark in Cà Mau, the southernmost city in Vietnam, directly across the Gulf of Thailand from Malaysia. If we could survive the crossing—250 miles of open ocean—we could apply for asylum as refugees in Malaysia.

After dark that night, I climbed silently back into the rickshaw with the Chinese family I had been staying with in Bạc Liêu. On my lap, I clutched my small duffel bag which held my few worldly possessions. We made the short drive to Cà Mau and once again were herded into another house. This one was crowded with 30-40 people, all waiting for the same boat. Every corner of the house was filled with people: men, women, and children, both Chinese and Vietnamese.

Once again, I settled into a strange house, this time hoping that my stay would be a much shorter one. The house was so cramped that there was no privacy. I kept to myself and made a place to sleep in one corner of the room. All I could do was wait and hope that the boat would indeed be ready soon.

***

Finally, on Saturday, March 13, 1979, everyone in the house was told that it was at last time to load the boat. After dark that evening, the whole assembly of people gathered their things. We were loaded into waiting rickshaws and driven along the dark, silent canals of Cà Mau. We stopped beside a dock on the Gành Hào River, the waterway that would take us out into the ocean. The boat was waiting, along with several local policemen. My heart seized. We were found out! The whole plan had worked this far, only to be thwarted at the dock!

But to my surprise, the police were there only to keep order and, like the soldiers at the checkpoints along the road, ensure that only ethnic Chinese were leaving the country. Once again, the smugglers reminded me to only use my fake Chinese name and a fake birthday which was printed on the forged documents.

Many times, this strategy had worked. By now, I had practiced my Chinese name so that I pronounced it as naturally as if it was my real name. But seeing that boat floating there in the dark water of the Gành Hào River, feeling so close to escape from Vietnam, I grew more anxious and nervous than I had felt in months.

I stepped from the vehicle and toward the water. The police officer asked my name and date of birth, which I gave to him in a voice I tried to force full of confidence. And once again, to my surprise and relief, the tired officer waved me on without so much as a second glance. Now, nothing but the boat and the dangerous crossing of the Gulf of Thailand lay before me. I stepped on board.

***

This was the first time I had set foot on a large boat, and I took a moment to look around me and take stock of it. The boat was a large wooden hull, about 25 meters long and maybe 10 meters wide. Toward the back of the open deck, there was a small pilothouse made of plywood. A wooden frame extended forward from the pilothouse, covered by plastic tarp which offered some shade and shelter. To my inexperienced eye, it seemed like a strong and well-built ship, and I felt a sense of relief in finally being on board after so many months of waiting and planning.

Already, the top deck of the boat teemed with people, and I was told to move down a set of wooden stairs to the lower level. This seemed fine to me; the night air was cool, and I assumed it would be warmer and safer down below. But as soon as I stepped down the stairs, I immediately wished to be back above.

Below deck, in the hold, were more than a hundred people, so closely packed together that there wasn't even enough room to walk among the crowd. People sat or squatted with their feet held close against their bodies. Clearly, the expectation had been set that each person should take up as little room as humanly possible in an effort to cram as many bodies into the space as it would hold. I tried to turn back up the stairs to the deck, but already more people were coming down behind me.

I found a small space among the masses and squatted there, wondering how long the voyage would last and whether we would remain crowded in this space for the entire duration.

About an hour later, the boat's engines began to rumble. Never in my life had I been down in the hull of a boat like this, and the new sensations sparked a fresh anxiety. The whole environment around me seemed like a living thing. The engines thrummed, and the sound reverberated off the timber frames around us. The faint odor of diesel fumes mingled with the stench of so many bodies packed into that hold. I felt the boat rock and sway beneath me, even in the relative calm of the river. Suddenly, I gained a new awareness of how precarious and helpless my situation was. There, on the other side of the boat's planking loomed the dark water of the Gành Hào River. If something went wrong, I realized—if a fire broke out or a leak—there would be no possibility of escape. Likely I would be trampled by the scores of people crammed against me in the mad rush for survival.

I did my best to put these thoughts out of my head. I tried to rest and think only of the fact that I had made it this far. I had escaped Vietnam and was on my way toward a new and unknown life.

***

After only about two or three hours of motoring down the Gành Hào River toward the sea, I heard the unmistakable sound of gunshots from above. Even in the engines' rattling din, those booming cracks made everyone in the hold jump and then freeze. We heard the engines slow to an idle and a voice say in Vietnamese that he was a representative of the Vietnamese government. The Coast Guard. We were caught.

I felt the boat roll beneath me and knew we must be turning around. The faces of my fellow refugees filled with confusion and fear. People murmured to each other. What did this mean? Where would we be taken now?

I knew that each person on that boat carried a story and a struggle as significant as mine. Each of us had sacrificed everything, had said goodbye to our families, had left behind every comfortable and familiar thing about our old lives for the hope of escape and a better future in a foreign land. The pervading question in the air was, *What now?*

The boat motored back up the river, escorted I was sure by an armed Coast Guard boat. Finally, the great rumbling of the engines shuddered and came to a stop. Angry voices from above ordered everyone off the boat.

Outside, the rising sun was cool and pink on the horizon. Men armed with machine guns escorted both the crew and refugees off the boat. They marched us in a single-file line back into the city of Cà Mau, away from the boat which had been my one hope of escape.

Our destination soon loomed into view: a military prison camp surrounded by a high, barbed-wire fence. Here was my future, I realized. I was now a prisoner. I would spend the unknown future locked up like an animal: possibly starved, possibly beaten, possibly killed. I might spend the rest of my life behind bars.

I clutched my small duffel bag to my chest as we marched over a steel bridge. I looked down into the brown, swirling water of the canal below me. Should I jump, I wondered. I was not a strong swimmer, but my time on the track team had left me with muscles and stamina. The future ahead of me held certain doom. If I jumped, perhaps there was a small chance of escape. But if I wasn't drowned or shot from above by one of the guards, then what? Here I was, sixteen years old, hundreds of miles from my home and family, alone in a strange city. Even if I managed to survive, where would I go?

All these thoughts of despair crossed my mind in the few seconds it took to cross that small bridge. Of course, I did not jump. I marched, following the line of prisoners ahead of me, pressed on by the mass of forlorn men, women, and children behind me. Through the iron gates of the prison camp we marched, into an uncertain life of detention.

***

Once in the camp, it quickly became clear that some kind of deal was being negotiated. Rumors circulated among our group that the Chinese men who had built and owned the boat were talking with the soldiers. Around four o'clock that afternoon, word spread that an agreement had been struck. The boat owners paid some large sum of gold—I have no idea how much—and that night, we would be allowed to leave Vietnam once more.

Around dusk, the soldiers roused us, and we began to march again. Only this time, we marched out of the prison. I could hardly believe it. Just hours before, I had been ready to throw myself off a bridge into the swirling waters of the river. I had resigned myself to the fact that I would spend months—maybe even years—imprisoned in this military camp. My hopes of escape from Vietnam already seemed a distant fantasy. But now I was marching again, back across the same bridge, back through the streets of Cà Mau to where the same boat sat waiting for us.

Once more, I followed the crowd of people down the stairs to the hold below deck. Somehow, it seemed as if there were even more people on the boat this time. Soon, the engines rumbled to life once more, and again we motored out of the sleeping city toward the open sea.

After two or three hours, I heard the sound of voices shouting from above, "The Coast Guard! The Coast Guard is chasing us!"

My first thought was that I must be dreaming. We were like a wounded mouse, and the communist soldiers an angry cat. Would they catch us and let us go over and over until the boat owners were drained completely of gold or we refugees died from exhaustion?

"Go! Go!" I heard from above. "Faster!"

The engines roared, picking up speed so that it seemed they might rattle the boat to pieces. I felt the hull pitching and rolling in the waves and knew we must be out of the river and into open water. The captain was trying to outrun the Coast Guard! If we could make it to international waters, we would have a chance of escaping, of crossing the Gulf of Thailand to the safety of Malaysia.

The boat continued for some time, bouncing and plowing at top speed through the waves I could not see. From below deck, I had no way of knowing whether the Coast Guard was gaining on us or how fast. Another powerless, nameless refugee in the hold of a boat, I could only wait and hope that we would make it.

Soon, the engines slowed, the roaring noise in the hold subsided, and the rolling motion of the boat increased somewhat. I heard cheers from on deck and knew the Coast Guard boat must have turned around. We had outrun the soldiers and entered international waters. Despite the false starts and incredible odds, I had escaped Vietnam! A wave of relief came over me. It seemed like nothing could stop our progress now. I began once again to try to imagine the strange, uncertain life that lay before me. In a new country, I would finish school. I would become an engineer or lawyer the way my parents had always hoped. I would make them proud and honor their sacrifice. All these thoughts played through my head as I drifted off to sleep in the cramped, stuffy hold. Little did I know that the trials and hardships of my journey had only just begun.

3. Survival at Sea

After outrunning the Vietnamese Coast Guard, our boat pointed its bow south across the Gulf of Thailand toward Malaysia. I didn't know how long the journey might last. I didn't even know how far the crossing was or what we were aiming for. Since then, I've learned that the shortest distance from the southern tip of Vietnam to Malaysia is approximately 250 miles. But, of course, we were not on the most direct route, which would likely bring us into contact with the authorities of various countries and pirates who frequently preyed on boats full of refugees. So, although I was unaware at the time, my boatmates and I had just embarked upon a crossing of more than three hundred miles of open ocean.

On the second day at sea, conditions in the hold below deck began to deteriorate. Already it was hot, muggy, and stinky from the sheer number of people crowded together in an unventilated place. With so many people in such a small area, there was nowhere to move to escape the cramped quarters. And there was no privacy. If you needed to urinate, you did so in a plastic bag and passed it along to your neighbors to be taken above and dumped overboard. To have a bowel movement, you were allowed upstairs and led to a small bathroom at the stern of the boat. Afterward, you returned immediately downstairs to the insufferable hold. These conditions were bad enough, but after two days at sea, people began to get seasick.

Now, in addition to bags of urine frequently being passed underneath your nose, there were thin plastic bags full of rancid vomit. And, of course, not all the vomit made it neatly into bags. The acrid stench now mingled with the already nauseating smell of sweat and body odor. All this only intensified the feeling of seasickness brought on by the constant rocking and swaying of waves. People began trying to lie down, trying to sleep, attempting to find some position that would alleviate their nausea. The once relatively orderly rows of people sitting and squatting now devolved into piles of humanity, limbs stacked and tangled among limbs in the sour-smelling filth.

The smell and stuffy closeness of the hold made me nauseous, but I was fortunate to discover that I'm not naturally predisposed to seasickness. I avoided the worst symptoms that some of my hold-mates experienced. Still, after two days, the sour smell became so strong that I could no longer stand it. I decided to go up on deck and try to somehow find a place for myself in the open air. I figured that as a lone, small boy without a family or traveling companions, I could unobtrusively find a space for myself. But as I climbed the stairs and felt the relief of the fresh ocean air, it became clear that the deck was completely jam-packed with people from one rail to the other. There was not even room for me to stand without pushing someone else out of the way. Only by squeezing between people and enduring their dirty looks and swears could I even move among them and make my way toward the small pilothouse at the back of the boat.

Through the windows of the pilothouse, I saw the gruff-looking men who operated the boat. One held the wheel, looking out over the tops of our heads to the open ocean beyond. Behind him, two men were bent over a navigation chart spread on a table. People jostled and pushed around me. Afraid I might be crushed against the pilothouse if I stood there much longer, I looked around for somewhere to escape. That's when my eyes drifted up and I saw the broad, flat top of the wooden, tarp-covered frame that served as a sunshade for the top deck. It seemed to me like a vast oasis, completely free from other passengers. If only I could make it up there!

I squirmed my way through the crowd to where the frame met the pilothouse. I was much too short to reach the edge of the roof, but my years of playing games in small spaces as a child, paired with my time on the track team, had left me strong and resourceful. I looked around for anything I could climb to boost myself onto the roof. By stacking an odd assortment of items, a pile of rope, a bucket, some pieces of wood, I managed to reach the edge and hoist myself up. And there, I found my oasis.

On top of the wooden frames, I was able to lie down on the plastic tarp. I stretched my limbs in all directions. It felt so good to have a private, uncrowded area where I could rest undisturbed. And the air! Even compared to the deck, the air tasted so sweet and fresh, with no twinge of vomit or sweat, only the salt of the sea and a bit of diesel exhaust from the boat's engines. I decided I would make the roof my home for the remainder of the boat's journey—however long that might be.

Soon, the sun drooped in the sky, and I marveled at the sunset in a way I never had. The expanse of ocean all around us was endless, no sight of land in any direction, as if the world existed only of water, sun, and our solitary boat full of terrified and nauseous refugees.

As the sun extinguished on the watery horizon, I began to realize the downside of my new home atop the roof. In the hold below, and even on deck, so many human bodies kept everyone warm—often too warm. But alone on the roof, the night air cut straight through my thin pants and shirt. Soon I was shivering. For a moment I considered climbing down into the warmth of bodies below. But I remembered the terrible stench and the cramped quarters with nowhere to lie down and stretch out. I resolved to bear the cold for the sake of having this small bit of privacy and space.

Because of the cold, sleep came in short and fitful intervals. When I couldn't sleep, I lay on my back on the roof and looked up at the blue-black sky. The boat's engine hummed from below, and the stars rocked with the motion of the waves. As a child, I had never paid much attention to stars. Rarely did I spend time outside after dark, and when I did, I occupied myself trying to find the latest game or avoiding my mother's admonishments. Now, for the first time, I had hours alone with nothing to do but watch the stars. Lying on my back, I became consumed by them, stars all the way from one horizon to the other, surrounding me in every direction. Shooting stars streaked across the heavens, inviting me to wish for a better future. It felt almost as if the boat did not exist below me. I could see nothing in my field of vision but stars swaying around me as if I had become unmoored and was floating alone in the vast emptiness of space.

I had plenty of time to think on these long, cold nights. I thought about my family and wondered if I would ever see my parents again. I tried to imagine circumstances that would make it possible. I also wondered what my life would be like outside Vietnam. I felt for the first time the weight of my entire life spread out before me. At 16 years old, I was still a child. If I survived this journey, I would live my whole life in a new country. Malaysia first, but then who knew where? France maybe. The United States. These places seemed as distant and fantastical to me as fairy tales. As hard as I tried to imagine my future in one of these foreign lands, I could not conjure a coherent vision. So I did my best to quiet my nervous mind. I allowed myself to drift with the stars above me, in and out of restless sleep.

***

During the day, I made it my duty to keep a lookout for passing ships. Each time someone spotted a dot or some shape on the horizon, a cry went up. We all hoped that it would be a ship that would take pity, rescue us, and deliver us to some safe port. A few times, a dark speck grew into a large oil tanker or container ship. They passed close enough that we were sure we'd been seen. But each time something appeared—whether a huge ship or a tiny speck among the vast expanse of blue—it passed us by without offering help.

I also kept a lookout for dark clouds that might threaten a storm. On top of the roof, I felt so exposed. My biggest fear was that a storm might come and capsize the boat. Any time I saw clouds gathering on the horizon, my stomach tightened with dread. Luckily, the weather remained fair and none of the clouds materialized into a squall.

Those first few days on the boat were a strange mixture of relief at having left Vietnam, uncertainty for the future, discomfort due to the crowded and unsanitary conditions, and wonder at the natural beauty of the sea. One time, I was scanning the horizon for ships and clouds when suddenly I heard a burst of air from somewhere in the water below me. I turned to see the sleek grey back of a dolphin disappear beneath the waves. No sooner had it vanished than another dolphin burst through the surface on the opposite side of the boat. Soon, an entire pod of dolphins was rushing ahead of our boat, leaping and playing in the waves curling off the bow. I had never seen anything so magnificent. I watched, mesmerized at the speed and agility of their movements.

On the third full day at sea, I spotted two dark specks far away on our stern side. Soon, all eyes on the deck were trained on these specks. They appeared to be growing larger, heading straight for our boat. I was ecstatic. We were saved! My feet would soon feel solid ground beneath them instead of the constantly swaying surface of the boat.

But my elation was short-lived. From my perch on the roof, I could sometimes hear the men in the pilothouse talking, and I heard someone say, "Those boats are pirates. We'd better be ready!"

When I heard that, I knew I had to warn the rest of the people on the boat. I leapt down from the roof and pushed my way through the crowded deck to the stairs which led down into the hold. I ducked in and yelled, "We're about to be met by pirates! Be ready!"

Of course, there was a great commotion after this, and the men on deck, sensing the tumult, began to shout, "Everyone stay calm! Don't panic! Don't move! If you panic, the boat will capsize!"

This was a real concern. So overloaded was the boat that its passengers could easily have swamped it by shifting all their weight to one side. Most people understood this, and so we did our best to remain calm and do what we could to prepare for the pirates.

I made my way downstairs to the hold I had abandoned for my home up on the roof. I felt so alert. Somehow, I knew exactly what I needed to do. The only items of value I had were a $50 bill which I had sewn into a hidden seam of my pants and a gold ring which I had worn on my finger since the moment I left my parents' house so many months ago.

I had never encountered sea pirates before, but I knew that this gold ring would attract attention. The small amount of gold was my only insurance policy against starvation on my journey. I had to keep it safe.

Down in the hold of the boat, I slipped the ring off my finger and wedged it into a tiny space between two boards, where the frame of the boat met the planking. Once the ring was hidden, I slipped up the stairs again. I didn't want to be stuck below the deck when the pirates arrived.

Now, we watched the two dots, which had once seemed so far away, grow larger and larger until their shapes became quite clear. Two boats, each maybe twice the size of ours, came into view, and they were charging toward us at full speed.

***

Before long, the boats overtook us. The first one slammed its heavy bow into our stern. I remember so distinctly the sickening sound of the wood cracking upon that impact. Screams rose from every corner of the boat as we were all thrown against each other by the force of the collision. This was it, I thought. Our boat was damaged, and now we'd all drown. The pirates would take what valuables they could from the floating wreckage.

It seemed there was some damage to the bathroom area at the stern of the boat. I imagined the water rushing in through the cracked boards, but miraculously, we remained afloat. The pumps in the engine room which spewed the excess bilgewater overboard must have been able to keep up.

The second pirate boat came to a stop alongside our starboard gunwale. Ropes were thrown across to lash our boat in place. Immobilized, trapped, surrounded by nothing but hundreds of miles of ocean, we were left at the pirates' mercy.

A handful of men came aboard from each of the two boats. Some held small fishing knives in their hands, but others had nothing more dangerous than a screwdriver. These were nothing but Thai fishermen, I realized. Maybe not hardened pirates, but opportunists enough to take advantage of a defenseless boat full of refugees from Vietnam.

They began searching the boat, demanding that all pieces of luggage be brought forward. They collected every suitcase, bag, and satchel on the boat and passed them over the gunwales to their own boats. There, other men began opening the luggage and searching through the bags and suitcases for any items of value. Sometimes they discovered jewelry; other times caches of money, family heirlooms, silverware, statues of the Buddha. Once emptied of these items, the clothes and toiletries were stuffed back into the luggage which was heaved back onto our boat.

Meanwhile, the pirates on our boat instructed everyone— in a combination of broken phrases and jabs with their knives—to form orderly single-file lines. Once everyone was lined up, the pirates walked among us, forcing everyone to show our hands, turn out our pockets, open our mouths. They searched each person from head to toe, once again confiscating everything they deemed of value.

For hours we stood helplessly while these pirates searched our belongings, our bodies, and our boat. Throughout the ordeal, I held an empty 50-liter plastic water container in my hand. I wanted something nearby that would offer a small amount of flotation if the boat capsized and we all ended up in the water. At times this outcome seemed likely as the pirates roughly shifted people and luggage about the boat to facilitate their search. I remember looking over the edge of the boat at one point into the blue-green water. A large fish circled the boat, feeding on some garbage and debris that had fallen overboard. I had almost no knowledge of the sea at that point in my life, but looking back, I can compare the shape of this long, sleek fish with what I now know. It was a shark.

As I stood there, watching the pirates rifle through our belongings and the shark circle our boat, I began to pray. My parents had always been devout Buddhists. As a child, they'd often taken me to our neighborhood pagoda. One of my frequent chores was to clean and care for the statue of the Buddha in our home. Once, they even took me to stay for three days at the Buddhist temple, thinking I might benefit from the discipline of the monks. But meditation and prayer never appealed to me. I had a hard time sitting still and was always much more interested in playing games.

Still, I remembered a prayer my mother had taught me to say to Phat Quan Am, the Compassionate Buddha. My mother always told me to pray to Phat Quan Am when I needed help. So in that moment, as I was considering whether I might jump into the ocean and drown or be killed by a pirate, I began chanting that prayer to myself.

As I prayed, I made a promise to the Compassionate Buddha. If I somehow survived this journey, I thought, I would dedicate my life to helping others. I would apply whatever skills I had to taking care of the sick and the poor.

The promise of that prayer remains with me to this day. Every day, I wonder whether I've yet fulfilled that promise.

And the memory of that moment has guided and informed nearly every major decision I've made in my life and career.

As I was praying silently to the Compassionate Buddha, the pirates approached to search me for valuables. I was grateful that I had planned ahead. The gruff, foul-smelling man patted down my pockets and made me open my hands and mouth, but he found nothing. The money sewn into my pants remained safely hidden. I only hoped that my ring would also escape detection between the boards in the hold below.

By the time the pirates finished their search of the boat, it was nearly dark. One of the pirates who spoke Chinese said a few words to the Chinese men operating our boat. Then they climbed back onto their ships, loosed the lines securing our boat, and motored away into the obscurity of dusk. Once they were gone, I made my way down into the hold and found my mother's gold ring, still safe in its hiding place. I slipped it back onto my finger.

Dealing with the pirates had been a frightening ordeal, but our boat was comparatively lucky. I had heard stories of pirates before, and I have heard more since. Robbery was often the least of their crimes. These part-time pirate-fishermen took their finds and left us mostly unscathed. They did not—as so many other pirates did when they came across a boat of helpless refugees—rape or take hostage any young women. No one was stabbed or shot or even injured. In an effort to keep everybody safe and alive, the men operating our boat encouraged everyone to comply with the pirates' demands. This we did, and together we made it through the ordeal of the pirates with only injuries to our boat. The bathroom at the stern was damaged where the pirates had rammed it, but it was still usable. There was also a big dent in the wood on the starboard side, but thankfully the wood had not cracked, and the boat remained afloat.

***

After the pirates left us, our boat continued its course toward Malaysia. Through the night and the next morning, we motored in that direction, our speed diminished by hull damage and strained bilge pumps. While listening to the captain and other men in the pilothouse the next day, I learned that we had entered Malaysian waters. We were getting close to shore and, hopefully, a friendly welcome from the Malaysian authorities.

This news came as a great relief. Looking down from the roof, I saw so many people in so much suffering. Sick, hungry, dehydrated, many had lost what few valuables they still possessed to the pirates. An overwhelming sense of despair lingered in the air over the mass of people strewn about the deck. It was our fourth full day on the ocean, and I knew there were some on board who would not survive if we did not soon reach the safety of shore.

I noticed one middle-aged couple that looked like they were in terrible shape. They were lying against the port-side gunwales of the boat. Their faces were pale, and they looked so weak that I was afraid they might die. As I was watching from the roof, I heard an old lady near them ask for a volunteer to help feed the couple. Hearing this, I climbed down, approached the couple, and asked the old lady how I could help.

The old lady gave me a small container of water and a spoon. "They need water," she said. "But not too much at a time."

For the next few hours, I sat beside the couple, spooning small amounts of water between their parched lips. When they seemed to be able to handle the water, I asked the people around me for some food. Someone gave me an orange, which I split in half, squeezing the juice into the couple's open mouths. Then, I fed them bits of meat and rice that someone gave me.

I could see the couple's condition improving as I sat with them. It gave me a tremendous sense of fulfillment and joy to see that I could be of service to these people. Already, I felt like I was making some progress toward fulfilling my promise to the Buddha.

As the couple recovered, they started talking to me. First, they thanked me for my help and then they started telling me a bit about themselves. They were both medical doctors, I learned. The man was a gynecologist, and the woman was a pediatrician. And there I was, a sixteen-year-old boy helping tend to these two doctors!

That moment was the first time I considered that I might pursue a career as a physician if I made it safely to a new country. The satisfaction I felt in helping these two people surpassed anything I had known before. From that point on, my old visions of a career as an engineer or lawyer never again appeared in my mind. As a doctor, I could help alleviate the suffering of people the way I had helped this couple. And I could fulfill the promise I'd made to the Buddha.

***

On the same day I sat with the two doctors, another dark shape appeared on the horizon. As it drew closer, it materialized into a large metal ship with cannons protruding ominously from its deck.

"Malaysian Coast Guard," I heard the captain say.

We are saved, I thought.

But my hope soon faded as the ship approached close enough for me to make out the shapes lining the deck railings. All the soldiers on board wore dark masks and held machine guns. This was not the friendly welcome I had been hoping for.

Over the loudspeaker from the Coast Guard ship came a message in a strange language (English, I later learned). I could not understand the words, but the meaning was clear from the tone and the reaction of our crew. *You are not welcome in Malaysia.*

The ship came closer. Waves from its massive hull rocked our little boat perilously. A soldier threw a large rope to one of our crew members, and it was fastened to our bow. Our engines rattled to a stop (though the pumps continued to run continuously in the hold), and the Coast Guard ship began towing us south, away from the Malaysian coast we had been aiming for.

For hours, all through that afternoon and into the evening, the Coast Guard ship towed our boat. Once, they sped up so much that our boat rocked violently back and forth. I held on to the edge of the roof frame to keep myself from being hurled overboard. Our captain started shouting, telling them to slow down, that we would capsize! But of course, the Coast Guard ship was too far away to hear our cries. People started screaming, and the captain shouted, "Cut the rope!"

With his knife, a deckhand hacked through the thick rope tied to our bow. We broke free, and our boat drifted to a stop. The Coast Guard boat continued motoring ahead for a few minutes, and I started to think that maybe they would abandon us. But they soon slowed, came about, returned to our boat, re-tied the rope, and began towing us again at a slightly slower speed.

The Malaysian Coast Guard towed our boat for over twenty-four hours. I had no idea where they might be taking us. Clearly, they had no intention of bringing us to their shores. They seemed to be dragging us out into the remote reaches of the open ocean. Not even the captain below me in the pilothouse seemed to know exactly what was happening. Everyone on board our boat existed in a state of stunned suspension during that long day and night. Meanwhile, the waves peeled away from our bow, the pumps in the hold churned to keep the seawater at bay, and our destination receded farther and farther into the distance.

The sun set, and the stars reignited in the darkening sky. This was our sixth night at sea. Atop the roof, I lay on my back and tried to keep my mind from despair. Our meager rations and freshwater had been depleted. Our boat had been ravaged by pirates. We were sick, dehydrated, sunburned, exhausted. And now, instead of moving toward some possible destination, toward some hope no matter how remote, we were moving farther away. Nearly a week we'd been adrift. I didn't know how many more nights we'd survive. I tried my best to quiet my fears, lay back on my rocking rooftop, and attempted to sleep.

Suddenly, I lurched awake. Out of nowhere, the boat had slowed drastically. I peered into the darkness ahead of our boat. Had we hit something? Had the Coast Guard run us aground on a shoal? But the sea lay as still and quiet as ever. In fact, everything seemed too still. Then I realized that our tow rope now dangled limply from the bow. The Coast Guard ship had cut us loose, and this time, it did not circle back for us. I watched the shadow of the large ship speed away into the darkness.

Where were we now? I had no way to tell. The oppressive blackness of the nighttime sea pressed in from all directions. Even if it had been broad daylight, one expanse of ocean looked indistinguishable to me from any other. But our captain seemed to know something of our location, or at least he was able to make a guess based on his compass and the position of the stars overhead. He ordered the engines started, and once more our little boat continued the journey under its own power. Though toward what destination now, I could not even begin to guess.

***

On the morning after the Coast Guard cut loose our boat, I awoke to a general hubbub from the passengers and crew below me. I soon realized that although we were motoring once more, we were moving much slower than we had been. I soon understood that our engines were struggling. The pumps could not keep up with the leaks in our damaged hull, and the encroaching seawater had begun to damage the engines. In short, our boat was sinking.

Every able-bodied man on board was told to start bailing water from the engine room. I leapt down from the roof and joined the line of men passing buckets of water from below, up onto the deck, and heaving them overboard.

For several hours I worked, passing the heavy buckets from the man on my left to the man on my right, and then passing the empty buckets back in return. The sun beat down on us, hot and oppressive in the humid ocean sky. The water seemed endless. It felt as if we were scooping water from the fathomless sea itself, only to empty our buckets overboard into that same ocean. I was among the strongest on board, my muscles and endurance toned by my time on the high school track team, and I volunteered to continue working even as the older men around me switched out with others waiting to take their place. But eventually, I grew too exhausted to continue. I passed a final bucket, sloshing its salty contents onto my sweat-drenched body, and nearly collapsed onto the deck.

Since meeting the pirates earlier in our voyage, food and water on board had been extremely scarce. But after seeing me work so hard, an older woman came over and offered me some water and a small amount of food. More than anything, I wanted water. Already, I was dehydrated—we all were—but after working for hours in the sweltering sun, my throat felt as dry and cracked as a desert full of scalding sand.

As I was lying there in my parched and exhausted state, I happened to look up and see an old woman crouched with her family in a nearby corner of the boat. I watched in horror and disbelief as she poured fresh drinking water into her hands and splashed it onto her face. At this sight, my own face seemed to grow ten degrees hotter. This old woman was washing her face! With freshwater! I would have done anything to drink the few precious drops which splashed uselessly off her skin onto the deck of the boat. I became so furious that I wanted to scream. I wanted to march across the boat and reprimand the woman for her thoughtlessness. But what could I do? I was so tired I could barely stand, and I realized—even in my fury—that this old woman and I were bound together by our circumstance. Whether any of us survived our journey depended entirely on the other people on board. Shouting at this woman would have accomplished nothing other than to make a scene. So I bit my tongue and stewed in my anger. I did my best to remain calm, even though to this day when I think of that woman splashing water on her face, it makes my throat ache with thirst.

After an hour or so of rest, someone tapped me on the shoulder and gestured back toward the line of bailing men. I took another shift passing buckets, working until my arms burned from exertion. And then, sometime during that second shift, I heard a cry from somewhere near the bow of the boat.

"Land! There's land ahead!" The excitement spread throughout the boat like electricity. There was land within sight! Soon we'd have solid ground beneath our feet!

For nearly a week, our boat had seemed like an isolated island, adrift, exposed to the elements of sun and sea, vulnerable to attack from pirates, and helpless before Coast Guard ships. After so long with nothing but the ocean, the sight of that dark line of land on the horizon was like the first glimpse of home after a long journey. But, of course, it was not home. For me and the other refugees on board that boat, the concept of home no longer existed. Our homeland had been decimated by decades of war and had fallen under the control of a government we neither trusted nor recognized. Months ago, I had left the only home I'd ever known. And yet, to a man who has spent a starving week at sea, the sight of any solid land is home.

Still, we had to reach that land, and this was no guarantee. For even as we paused for a few moments to celebrate the first sight of shore, the water continued to pour into our boat through the damaged hull. Land was still many miles away, and our engines struggled now more than ever. I returned to the work of passing buckets while the boat slowly limped toward what appeared to be an island, growing steadily larger before us.

By the time we neared the island, our engines were truly on their last legs. They stuttered and sometimes stopped completely for horrible minutes at a time before being restarted and allowing us to slowly make our way closer to land. Finally, the voice of the captain came shouting over the noise of the boat.

"Who on board can swim? Someone needs to swim ashore with a rope to pull us in!"

I raised my head to look overboard toward the island. Between us and the sandy beach lay a maze of shallow coral reefs and crashing waves. I didn't even know how to swim. There was no I way I would volunteer for a crazy job like that one!

The captain shouted again, "Someone has to swim to shore!" He looked left and right among the crowd, and when no one volunteered, the captain cursed and ducked his head back into the pilothouse.

Now, the boat turned and headed directly toward the nearest point of land—aiming directly into the shallow reefs. I realized then that this would be no brief layover. The captain intended to run our already damaged boat directly into the island. These would be our last moments aboard this boat. We would not be leaving under our own power.

Seconds later, I heard the crunch of our hull impacting the coral reef, and I was thrown to the deck along with the men who had been bailing water around me. The engines below us sputtered one final time and then died. The captain's head reemerged from the pilothouse, and he shouted, "We need to be pulled to shore!"

This time, several men jumped to his call. They lowered themselves over the side of the boat, standing on the coral reefs in chest-deep water. The coral was jagged and sharp, but the men managed to grab ahold of ropes attached to the boat's bow and made their way to the sandy beach. Once on solid ground, they used the ropes to haul the boat up onto the beach. When the hull was lodged in the coral reef, as far ashore as it would go, the captain ordered everyone off the boat.

My suspicions were confirmed when, as people clambered off the boat clutching their few belongings, the captain began ordering men to dismantle the hull and disable the engines. "As quickly as possible!" he said. "We don't want anyone to come along and tow us back out!"

I understood his strategy. Survival on this island was not a guarantee, but if the Coast Guard returned and towed our damaged boat back out into the ocean, we would surely sink and drown.

I quickly found my black duffel bag, made sure my mother's gold ring was securely on my finger, and then I climbed over the side of the boat and waded through the shallow water onto the beach. I dropped my luggage there and returned to the boat to help remove anything that might be useful to our survival. As I was returning to the boat, I saw the family I had stayed with in Saigon and Cà Mau, the three sisters and their children. I decided that I should try to stay with them—to help them in any way I could and hopefully benefit from being part of a family group. I helped them unload their luggage from the boat and found a few small bags of rice. I recruited some of the children to help me carry the rice to shore.

Within a few hours of disembarking our boat, the men had completely disassembled it. Planking hung from the frames, and daylight could be seen through the sides and deck. It no longer resembled a functional boat so much as the carcass of some enormous sea monster, washed up and rotting on the beach.

As the sun began to blush the western sky over the calming ocean, I looked around me. People had dragged themselves up the beach to the shade of palm trees where they clustered into small groups. A few attempted to build fires. Others simply huddled against each other, staring blankly at the sea. We had survived the ocean journey, if barely. But we had not reached a destination. And now, stranded on this small, remote island, a new phase of survival would begin.

4. Island Life

That first night on the island, I stayed close to the family I had been with back in Vietnam, the three sisters and their children. In some ways, it felt good to be back among familiar faces. But at the same time, I was acutely aware of my status as an outsider, just as I had been in their home in Saigon and their brother's house in Bạc Liêu. Those months we had spent waiting for the boat to be ready seemed like an eternity ago, even though we'd left the house in Bạc Liêu less than two weeks earlier.

The women set a small pot of water over an open fire and began cooking some of the rice I had found. Meanwhile, I tried to make myself as unobtrusive as possible, just as I had when living in their house in Vietnam. I sat a short distance away from the bubbling pot, listening to the murmur of the women's voices and their children.

The next morning, I explored the island along with a few other men from the boat. It didn't take long. The island was only about 150 meters across and appeared to be completely uninhabited except for our group of about 350 refugees washed ashore and now marooned. Our best discovery turned out to be a small stream which leaked out a slow trickle of freshwater near the island's center. This small stream, modest though it was, allowed us to refill the 20-liter plastic water containers from the boat. We boiled this water for drinking, and for the first time since leaving Vietnam, I was able to drink my fill.

We remained on the island for four or five days, subsisting off the stream's freshwater, the remaining rice and rations from the boat, and meat from the coconuts that grew on the island. Then, one afternoon, some Indonesian villagers from a nearby island arrived in a small boat. They must have seen smoke from our fires and come to investigate. This confirmed what many people from our boat had suspected: the Malaysian Coast Guard had towed us away from their country and into Indonesian waters. Overwhelmed by the influx of refugees, they had passed us off to a neighboring country.

The Indonesians disembarked onto our beach and handed out some small packages of cookies. The bright, colorful plastic wrapping stood out after so many days of rice and canned food. And the flavor was even better. I savored those few mouthfuls of sweetness as if I'd never tasted anything better.

The Indonesian men spoke in English to some of the crewmembers who'd been in charge of our boat. I had no idea what they were saying, but I hoped they were negotiating some deal to get us off this island. I turned out to be correct, though not in the way I expected.

The Indonesians left and returned the next day with another, slightly larger boat. Our group was told to get onto this boat, and we would be taken off the island. I felt such relief. Finally, I thought, after all our trials someone was taking pity on us and offering help. I assumed they would take us to a UN refugee camp where we would be cared for and eventually resettled. But I was wrong. Instead of bringing us somewhere safe, the Indonesians simply transported us to another nearby island and deposited us there so that the local authorities could keep a closer eye on us.

It's difficult for me to explain the feelings I had during this time. I was so exhausted, mentally and physically, that I had little energy for reflection. The Indonesian people did not abuse or mistreat us. They politely explained that we would be moved to this new island. We had no choice but to go along with them.

It's easy to say that you would never allow yourself to be treated in such a manner. Maybe you believe you would demand help. Or you think that you could never find yourself in a situation like this one. It's easy to say, I would never give up. I would keep fighting no matter what. But after nearly two weeks of physical and mental exhaustion, I felt ready to give in. I began to wonder if I had made the right decision. Perhaps it would have been better to stay in Vietnam to help my parents and siblings eke out their scarce existence under the communist regime. Perhaps I would have been drafted into the army to fight against Cambodia. Perhaps I would have been killed in battle.

These were my thoughts as I stood on a second foreign beach, watching the Indonesian boat grow smaller and smaller in the distance until it disappeared over the heartless blue horizon.

That first evening on the second island, I helped set up a makeshift camp with the three sisters and their families. From the beach where we'd been dropped off, we carried our few supplies up a small incline to a flat spot among a grove of coconut trees and shrubby bushes. I did my best to be helpful, clearing space, gathering firewood, and carrying rice, clothing, and luggage up from the beach.

The women started cooking dinner, and I stuck around to be helpful. Then, the oldest of the sisters brought out an aluminum can of meat to add to the pot of rice. With a start, I realized it was the same can of dry, shredded pork that my mother had given me before I left home. My emergency rations which I had saved all this time! I didn't know how she'd found the can—whether she had stolen it from my luggage or whether I had set it down somewhere while moving things from the boat. I bit my tongue and watched her add it to the food.

When the meal was ready, she called me over and offered me a bowl of rice with *my* pork! It took everything in my power not to accuse her of stealing my supplies. But I did not. I simply accepted the food and ate in silence.

Whether it was intentional or not, this gesture reinforced the fact that anything else of value I possessed now belonged to this family. I no longer had any control. This frustrated me, but what could I do? Staying with this family offered my best chance of survival. Alone, I would be cut off from even these meager supplies. I might be subject to theft or attack from other desperate people on the island. There was safety and utility in being part of a group—even if it was one I could not fully trust.

That night, I lay down to sleep under the stars next to a fallen coconut tree. Even though my body was exhausted, I couldn't sleep. I sat in the dark, listening to the sound of the ocean and watching its endless dark expanse. I didn't know how long we would be forced to live on this remote island, whether I would ever be free of the family I felt indebted to, or whether I would ever make it to France or the United States to begin a new life.

***

The next morning, I learned more about the new island we'd arrived on. It was much larger than the first island, but there was no freshwater stream running down the hillside from which to gather drinking water. Instead, the island was separated from an even larger island by a shallow stretch of water about 2 kilometers across (roughly 1 ¼ miles). About 300 Indonesian villagers lived on the larger island, and they maintained a small market. Sometimes at low tide, the spit connecting the two islands dried out completely, and it was possible to walk across to reach the larger island. Other times, the low tide only reached about thigh-deep and we could wade through the shallow. In this way, our little community of castaways was able to collect freshwater and set up a system of trade with our neighbors.

Each day at low tide, a small contingent of men from our group would walk or wade across to the larger island to collect water and barter for food and supplies. Of course, many of our valuables had been stolen by the pirates at sea, but like me it seemed many people had managed to hide small amounts of money and jewelry which now formed the basis of our makeshift economy.

Nearly every day, I joined the group that crossed the spit to the main island. The area between the two islands was full of small rock caves and holes in the ocean floor. Wading across in my bare feet, I had to avoid the little fish that would come out and nibble at my feet. It became a kind of game, like running across a field full of traps. Going across to the larger island gave me an excuse to escape the controlling eyes of the three sisters—to whom I was still shackled—and provided some structure to my life on the island.

Our group of stranded refugees settled into a routine of survival living, and I began to have increasingly bitter disagreements with the family I had attached myself to. Along with the three adult sisters, there were nine children, three girls and six boys, ranging in age from nine to sixteen. The husbands of the oldest and youngest sisters had disappeared during the war, but the middle sister's husband, a nurse, was there with us on the island. In addition, there were three small children whose parents had not been on the boat with us. Since they had no one to look after them, I had taken them into my care somewhat, making sure they had enough food and that they were safe.

The family of the three sisters made their expectations of me clear. The older children helped with some of the chores, but just like when I was staying in their house in Vietnam, the bulk of the work fell to me. I carried water, foraged for firewood, built fires, constructed shelters, dug holes for latrines, and cleaned up after everything the family did.

Sometimes I did this work willingly, knowing that my fate—and my access to food—depended upon this family. But sometimes I complained. It has never been in my nature to be quietly submissive. My childhood penchant for mischief manifested itself now in wondering aloud why the other boys never did the same amount of work as me. Any time I voiced a sentiment like this, one of the women would invariably hear and chastise me. They called me such names! Ungrateful! Lazy! Useless!

One of the girls picked up on this theme and started berating me, using foul language and saying terrible things about my family. Once, the middle sister overheard me grumbling about her daughter's language and the unfair workload. She stood up from where she was squatting by the fire and slapped me hard across the face.

"I have to take care of my family first!" she said, her voice seething with anger. "You are second. You are with us in order to survive, but you are not part of this family!"

After that I learned to keep my mouth shut, at least when I was within earshot of the sisters. I obediently did the work I was told to do. If I had doubted it before, the woman's words made it clear how little this family actually cared for me. My survival could be put in jeopardy if I did not obey.

Some of the men from our boat helped the three sisters build a small tent on the flat space they'd claimed the first night on the island. Their family could sleep under this rudimentary cover and be out of the weather. I helped build the shelter, but once we'd completed it, I was told I wouldn't be allowed to sleep there. When I asked why, one of the older children told me that the oldest sister was afraid I would rape one of the girls if I was allowed in the tent. This infuriated me. I had been nothing but a helpful and respectful companion on our arduous voyage. Had I ever shown any tendency toward violence? Never in my life, and certainly not here among other survivors. But these women never trusted me. No matter what I did, I was always an outsider, treated as nothing more than a servant.

Since I was not allowed in the tent, I found a bush nearby, and like an animal, I carved out a little hole underneath. At night, I would curl up beneath the bush with a small cotton blanket that I'd brought with me in my luggage. The blanket and the bush's foliage offered some warmth and protection from wind and weather. Like the roof of the boat, that bush became my home, my small place of privacy and refuge.

During the day, I watched over the children, making up games for the little ones like I used to play in my parents' store. Even after the way the family had treated me, I felt obligated to help them. The three sisters had, after all, been the ones who had helped my family coordinate my escape. If not for them, I might have still been in Vietnam. And so I continued to do the daily chores. I hauled water from the larger island. I traded and scrounged for food. I gathered firewood and chopped down dead trees for cooking fuel. I helped cook rice and prepare meals. I did everything I could to make myself useful and contribute to our strained partnership.

***

I had no idea how long we would be stranded when we arrived on the second island. It turned out that we spent four months living in this way. Each day a struggle. Each day a challenge to compile the necessities of survival from the meager materials on hand. During this time, I grew up very quickly. From carrying water and supplies back and forth across the sandy spit, the muscles of my arms and legs hardened and bulked. I became extraordinarily strong and physically fit. But working so hard, burning so many calories, also left me ravenous with hunger. And that feeling never left me for the duration of our stay on the island. The three sisters and their family shared what food they had with me—in that way they were generous—but there was never quite enough to go around, and their children always ate first.

It was on the second island that I dipped into my emergency survival plans. I still had with me my mother's gold ring, and during one trip to the market on the larger island, I sold it for a small amount of cash. This, along with the $50 bill I had sewn into the seam of my pants, allowed me to buy a little bit of food each morning when I crossed over to the larger island to collect water.

Since I visited the market nearly every day, I got to know many of the food vendors and other people who lived on the larger island. I learned a bit of the Indonesian language, and soon I could communicate in a rudimentary way with the locals. One family in particular seemed to take pity on me.

It started with a young woman whom I met one day while collecting freshwater.

She approached me with a smile and said, "Your shirt has so many holes in it. I think you need a new one."

I laughed because this was the only shirt I owned, and I'd been wearing it for weeks on end. What little money I had, I spent on food and supplies. A new shirt seemed like an extravagant luxury—one I could never afford.

I assumed she was only being polite, offering the small kindness of sympathetic words. But after meeting her a few times, she invited me to her home. I followed her along the road between the market and the freshwater spring. Her family's house was very simple, but compared to the bush I slept under, it seemed like a palace. The house consisted of a simple one-room wooden structure built on stilts over the water with a wooden gangway that led to the beach. The bathroom was a wooden plank in the floor which could be lifted up to reveal a hole. Each day the receding tide washed the waste away.

At her house, the woman presented me with a fresh, clean shirt. It was a short-sleeved button-up with a pink pattern and lavender birds swooping across it. It's difficult for me to overstate the value of that present and the gratitude I felt in that moment. My old shirt had been tattered by weeks of ocean wind, sand, and salt. There were holes along the neck and seams, and the thread holding it together seemed to be disintegrating bit by bit each day. A new shirt made me feel like a new man, not a refugee or a castaway, but a dignified, normal person.

Nearly forty years later, I still have that shirt with me today. I can take it out of its drawer, hold the fabric in my hands and vividly remember the heartwarming smile on the woman's face when she first handed it to me. The memory of that kindness will stay with me for the rest of my life.

***

After receiving the shirt, I frequently saw the woman at the market or along the road, and as my understanding of the Indonesian language developed, we became friends. Sometimes, she invited me back to her house to share a small meal with her family.

The woman's husband was a fisherman. Every morning, he would set out in a very skinny wooden boat and return in the afternoon with fresh fish for the family to eat. The woman also had a younger sister who was about my age. She had large, kind eyes and long, beautiful eyelashes. She was quick to laugh and seemed excited to talk with me. Sometimes, after a meal of fresh fish with the family, she and I would have time to play together. We would talk in a combination of broken Indonesian and hand gestures and laugh at our often-futile attempts to make sense of each other's words.

***

One day, after sharing a morning meal with the family, the woman said to me, "You don't have to go back to that other island tonight. Why don't you stay here with us?"

Her offer caught me off guard. The woman and her family had already been so generous and welcoming. I was indebted to them for their kindness. I did not want to impose myself on them further. I thanked her and politely declined.

But she did not give up so easily. "You could live here with us," she said. "We have plenty of space, and it would be helpful to have you around. You don't have to be lost anymore."

For a moment, I hesitated. I allowed myself to imagine what my life might look like living there with that family. The kind woman and her hard-working fisherman husband. Her beautiful, playful sister, already my friend. We would no doubt grow closer. Perhaps I would marry her and have children. We would live a simple existence in one of these stilt houses, taking only what we needed from the ocean and trading for the rest in the market. I was tempted to say yes.

But I remembered why I had left Vietnam. I had not fled my home and left my family only to end up on a remote Indonesian island a few hundred miles away. My parents had sacrificed and risked so much in order to help me escape Vietnam. I had to stick with my plan to reach France or the United States and begin a new life. I would work hard and become an engineer, a lawyer or a doctor like my parents always imagined. Then I would be able to send money back to Vietnam to help my family, and I would fulfill my promise to the Compassionate Buddha to help other people.

I looked into the warm, open face of the woman, thanked her profusely and said no, I could not live there with them. I had my own path to follow, wherever that might lead.

***

The Indonesian family were not the only friends I made during that time. Back on the smaller island, my days were filled with chores and taking care of the smaller children. At night, I returned to my hollowed-out bush to rest and gather my thoughts, reflecting back on the day's events and my hopes for the future.

Nearby, another man had also created a makeshift shelter from bushes and branches. At first, we simply acknowledged each other with a nod or a small hello. But after several nights of sleeping in such close proximity, we started to have occasional conversations. I learned that his name was Hai and that he had been the Vice-Secretary of Finance for the South Vietnam government before the communist North Vietnamese took over.

Hearing his story made me realize how little I knew about my fellow refugees. I had assumed that most of them were like me, regular people who had scrimped and saved in order to afford this small chance to find a better life. But I understood now that many of the people on the boat with me had come from prominent and wealthy families. Those who had held positions of authority and privilege under the South Vietnamese government were the most likely to be targeted by the new communist regime.

My family had always been relatively poor. I grew up used to sleeping in cramped and crowded spaces and using my own ingenuity to get by. The idea that I would find myself living this way seemed somehow fathomable. But here was the

Vice-Secretary of Finance, a man who had once met President Nixon and who had helped make official state policy, now sleeping under a bush!

We soon became good friends. To occupy ourselves and keep our minds off the constant discomfort and hunger, we had wide-ranging conversations. Looking out on the ocean with our feet in the sand, he taught me about the world of finance, interest rates, international monetary flow, and economic theory. Through him, I gained access to a world of knowledge I never knew existed. So much of the world's suffering and strife, it seemed, came down to the simple fact of resources inefficiently distributed.

***

For four months, I lived this way. Each morning, I crawled out from under my bush and made the crossing to the larger island—sometimes walking, sometimes wading, and sometimes swimming. On the larger island, I gathered water and traded for food in the market. Often, I met my Indonesian friends—the caring woman with her beautiful sister—and spent some time with them. Upon returning to the small island, my life consisted of service to the three sisters and their families. I gathered firewood and cleaned their campsite. I helped prepare our meager meals. After completing the household work, my job was to watch over and entertain the smaller children.

Daily survival on the island presented an exhausting challenge. And yet, people are so resilient. I soon settled into a routine, and although I was constantly tired and hungry, the tedium of work superseded any big questions about life and death. That is, until one event reminded me of just how vulnerable our existence had become.

One evening, as people were settling into their sleeping places, I heard a terrible scream rise up from the direction of the three sisters' tent. I ran over to see what had happened, assuming someone had injured themselves. There in the tent lay one of the children, one of the youngest sister's boys. Writhing in pain, he clutched at his stomach and screamed like a wild animal. I stood by helplessly, unsure what to do.

After a few minutes, the boy seemed to calm down a bit, and he lay still for a while. But then, another child in the tent, an eleven-year-old boy, began to wail and hold his stomach. Clearly, they had eaten something bad and were experiencing some kind of poisoning.

It wasn't long before the second boy started convulsing and vomiting. By now a small crowd of people had gathered around the tent, drawn by the screaming and commotion. A man stepped forward and identified himself as a doctor. Here was another reminder of the former prominence of the people on our boat. Like the finance secretary, this man had enjoyed a position of respect and authority in our old society. But here, his face had blended into the helpless mass of refugees on our boat.

Three more men who said they were doctors also crowded in to help. I felt relieved. These men could help. They had expertise and training. I marveled at the confidence the doctors exuded and the deference shown to them by the three sisters.

One doctor started doing chest compressions, while another gave mouth-to-mouth resuscitation to the boy. A third doctor gave directions to people around him. He told me to massage the boy's legs, to help blood circulate through the body. I did the best I could, holding the boy's limp leg in my hands and working the tissue. If I stopped for even a few seconds, the skin beneath my fingers turned cool.

After an hour of continuous CPR, the doctors' shirts were soaked with sweat, and the situation seemed hopeless. I believe now that the doctors knew there was nothing they could do to help the child, but they continued doing CPR anyway, taking turns to relieve each other, to show the boy's mother that every effort was made to save her child.

Exhausted, one doctor turned to the group of bystanders. "We need help," he said. "Is there a strong swimmer who can go to the other island for help?"

By that time, I had been making the trip across the channel to the larger island every day for months, but never in the middle of the night. And never at high tide. I stood up and looked across the dark expanse of water that separated us from the larger island where there was a medical clinic. I was not a strong swimmer, but I volunteered to go. I knew how to speak a few words of the Indonesian language, and I figured I could make it across by using an empty plastic water container for flotation. I started to turn to run for help. But just as I was leaving, the doctor changed his mind.

"No," the doctor said. He stopped compressing the boy's chest and sat back on his heels. "It's too late."

In the dark, I could not see the boy's face, and it was

difficult for me to fathom that this small, limp form at my feet was the same boy I'd been playing with earlier that day. But of course, it was him. There was no escaping the cold fact of the moment: the child had died. The doctor reached down and pulled a blanket over the boy's face.

The boy's mother, oldest of the three sisters, had been watching the whole ordeal in a kind of stunned silence. But as soon as the doctor stopped performing CPR, and the reality of death settled over the group, she began crying hysterically. Coming from a culture that did not often display emotion, such an outpouring of unrestrained grief startled and terrified me. This was the same woman who had coldly banished me from her family shelter and treated me like a servant. But clearly there was intense love for her family within her—a love which had now transformed to anguish.

My friend the finance secretary, a second man, and I waited for the tide to recede early the next morning, then we crossed the channel to the larger island. There, we asked the villagers if we could use a piece of land to dig a grave for the boy. They pointed us to a sloping patch of hillside on the edge of town where there were other graves. With borrowed shovels, we worked for several hours to dig a large, deep hole for the body. When we were finished, we wiped the sweat from our foreheads, and some villagers who had been watching us somberly approached and gave us some food and water. For the first time in my life, I felt like a beggar. Even though we had not asked for food, the villagers saw how exhausted and hungry we looked, and they took pity on us. It was a small gesture, but I appreciated it immensely. Their simple act of charity showed that we were not entirely alone. The villagers sympathized with our grief and loss, and this was their way to communicate those feelings.

The death of the boy changed the mood on the island for everyone. On our long journey, people had often been sick, dehydrated, and malnourished. But up to that point no one had died. To witness a child's death, and to realize that even in the event of such a critical emergency no one had come to our aid, crystallized the severity of our situation in a way that nothing else had.

The most drastically changed among us, however, was the boy's mother. She had been strict and cruel to me from the beginning, but after her son's death, she became even more protective and controlling. Rarely did she let her remaining son and daughters out of her sight. And the more protective she became, the worse she treated me. I always understood that I was an outsider among their family, that they only tolerated my presence out of some sense of duty to my family and because I was helpful in looking after the children and doing chores. But now the oldest sister felt no shame in telling me exactly how she felt.

"I have to protect *my* family," she told me. "You are not my family, and I can't be expected to help you."

What could I say in response to this? What she said was true. And always there was more work for me to do. I had no choice but to continue working. And so I did my best to continue my routine: carrying water, preparing food, chopping wood, and making myself useful to a family that saw me as disposable.

***

After the first two months on the island, more refugees started to arrive in boats of various shapes and sizes. Some, like ours, had been shipwrecked on other islands, and the Indonesians moved the survivors to our island. But increasingly, boats full of refugees were being towed directly to our island and their passengers abandoned there with us.

Our original group of 352 people soon grew to 1000. Still more refugees arrived. Within a few weeks, 1000 grew to 1500. And then 2000. The island became so crowded that we developed serious issues with sanitation and cleanliness. From the beginning, everyone was told to defecate into the ocean where the tide would wash the waste away. But apparently there were now people on the island who didn't want to get wet. Possibly they were afraid of the ocean after their harrowing journey by boat. Whatever the reason, human waste began to accumulate between rocks by the shore and on a small hill near the center of the island. Meetings were called to address the issue, but it seemed to have little effect.

Flies became a problem. The stench of our island must have attracted them from the larger island. Or maybe they multiplied quickly in the newly fetid conditions. Soon, there were more flies than I had ever seen before. Flies were everywhere, constantly buzzing around my ears and crawling on my skin. When I tried to eat, I had to scoop my food with one hand and brush flies away with the other to avoid eating mouthfuls of insects.

Of course, with flies and unsanitary conditions also came more disease. The oldest sister's surviving son developed Hepatitis A. He had a fever, diarrhea, and terrible abdominal pain. Once, I walked past the tent and caught a glimpse of the boy lying on a tarp. His skin had an unnatural yellow hue from jaundice. The sisters were terrified that they would lose another child, and they sat up with him at all hours, berating me or anyone else who came near to offer comfort or help.

Eventually, the boy recovered, but the tension and conditions of the island did not improve. Each day, it seemed, someone else fell sick. And still more boats arrived, crowding the island well beyond any sanitary capacity.

And then one day, as if out of the blue, I heard the distinct thundering of a helicopter descending onto our island. The bright white flanks of the machine were emblazoned with two bold, black letters: UN.

The helicopter landed on the beach amid a spray of sand. A group of soldiers stepped out and talked to some men from our boat who spoke English. Word spread quickly across the island. The United Nations High Commission on Refugees had somehow learned about the overcrowded makeshift settlements on our island and the other small islands nearby. They planned to evacuate us to a nearby official refugee camp where we could apply for refugee status and resettlement.

At last—six months after leaving my home in Saigon, after one week at sea and four months surviving on a remote island—help had finally arrived.

5. A New Life in the United States

Things moved quickly after the UN helicopter disappeared back into the blue sky above the beach. Within a few days, a boat arrived, ready to take us away from the island that had been our home for the past four months. A rumor spread that someone had tried to bribe the UN officials for first priority to leave the island, but luckily the soldiers decided to evacuate people in the order they had arrived. Since my boat had been there the longest, we were the first to leave. I, along with the three sisters and their families, my friend the finance minister, and the other 351 refugees from our boat, waded into the shallows of the beach and once again climbed aboard a strange boat, clutching our few ragged belongings.

Looking back at the island as the boat motored away into the open ocean, I felt a complex mixture of emotions. On one hand, I was overjoyed to be leaving that filthy, desolate island and moving closer—I hoped—to my goal of reaching France or the United States. But with each life transition, it's difficult not to look back on the past with some fondness, regardless of how trying the time might have been. I thought about the kind-hearted woman on the large island who took pity on me at the market. Her kindness, and that of her family, had made my time on the island more tolerable and had given me hope to continue. I regretted that I had not been able to say goodbye or had the opportunity to adequately thank them for helping me survive. As the island faded into the distance and the sun sank lower on the horizon, I said a private word of thanks to that family and then turned to look forward, toward whatever new challenges lay before me.

***

The boat the UN used to transport us was a large Indonesian fishing vessel. We motored for a full day and night until we reached the city of Tanjung Pinang, Indonesia. After living for months on a remote island, stepping off the boat into a bustling city was a disorienting experience. As the boat approached the shore, I saw mopeds and cars rushing along the streets. My heart raced with excitement. Thousands of Chinese and Indonesian local people moved about the port, readying boats for fishing and loading goods to be transported to various other islands.

We were led from the boat by local police into a large refugee camp on the edge of the city. Barbed wire surrounded the perimeter, and armed guards stood at the only entrance. Walking through the gates reminded me of the military camp in Vietnam where the Coast Guard had taken us so many months ago. Once again, I had the urge to flee. It seemed I was simply being herded from one prison to the next. Once again, I had no way of knowing how long I would be forced to live behind the gates of this facility, but I had no choice. If I ran, I might be shot by one of the guards. Even if I escaped, I wouldn't be able to live there in Indonesia. A lone Vietnamese boy would stick out as an obvious refugee, and no doubt I would be returned immediately to the camp. So, I held my deteriorating black duffel bag tightly and walked silently through the gates.

Inside the refugee camp loomed several large buildings designated as places to sleep. They consisted of a single open room lined with rows of wooden benches. Guards assigned each person a small section of bench to call their bed. The toilet and bathing area, located in another building about one hundred yards away, consisted of a long row of toilet holes with buckets and water for washing. The conditions were spartan but clean, and after four months sleeping in the sand under a bush, a wooden bench and a blanket and a roof over my head felt luxurious. Every few days, the guards distributed food rations—canned vegetables or sardines with rice or chow mein noodles. Once per week, refugees were allowed to leave the camp through the checkpoint to buy goods in the city. By this time, I spoke Indonesian quite well, and I happily went to the market to trade. It felt good to be a part of civilization and not to have to forage for supplies or firewood the way we had on the island.

Even though I was living behind barbed wire, I felt a sense of freedom in the refugee camp that I had not felt since leaving Saigon. The three sisters and their families had come to the camp with me, but I no longer felt indebted to them. They had helped me secure passage on the boat from Vietnam, and for that I was grateful. For the past several months, I had done all I could to work for them and help them survive. I felt that my debt had been repaid, and I was happy to escape the judgement and overbearing criticism of the sisters. Honestly, I think they felt the same way. They were glad not to feel responsible for my well-being anymore. When we saw each other in the refugee camp, we exchanged polite greetings, but we no longer associated closely with one another. From that point on, I was on my own.

**

My first priority upon reaching the refugee camp was to try to send word to my family in Saigon that I had survived. My older brother had escaped by sea just a few months before me, and my family had known many people who had left Vietnam by boat the way we had. When someone left, their family waited to hear word of their crossing. It was generally accepted that if a family did not receive a telegram after two or three weeks, it was likely that they had drowned at sea. In my case, several months had passed since I left Vietnam. I was certain that my family assumed the boat had sunk and I had drowned. I was anxious to let them know I was alive.

Much later, I learned that my mother sat each day on the cement stairs of my uncle's house, waiting for the mailman, hoping for a telegram with news about my fate. But after months without any word, she began to feel guilty for sending me on such a perilous journey. She prayed fervently at the

Buddhist temple, asking for a miracle—some indication that I was alive.

However, sending a message was not straightforward. Escaping Vietnam in the way I had was, of course, illegal. The communist Vietnamese government did not want to encourage the outflow of refugees, so they had essentially cut off communications with nearby countries like Malaysia and Indonesia. This made it impossible to send a telegram directly from the refugee camp to my family in Saigon. However, a system had been established to circumvent this barrier. In Europe, there was a sizable population of people sympathetic to Vietnamese refugees. Some were family members or friends who had already been resettled abroad; others were kind European citizens doing what they could to help refugees they would never meet, strangers living on the other side of the world. By sending a telegram to one of these people in Europe, with instructions to forward the information, it was possible to send a message to family members in Vietnam.

In this way, I sent a message to my family letting them know that I had survived the journey and was awaiting my fate, along with thousands of other refugees in Indonesia. I knew not to hope for a reply. It was unlikely that a telegram would reach me in the sea of anonymous humanity I was caught up in. At that time, I didn't even know my brother and sister's fate. For all I knew, they were still in Malaysia. I had heard that resettlement could take months, even years. All I could do was wait.

But, as it turned out, I didn't have to wait very long at all.

**

At the time, several Western countries had begun accepting refugees, including the United States, France, Canada, and Australia. From the beginning, my goal was always to reach France. Vietnam had once been a French colony, so I was familiar with the culture and knew that many Vietnamese families had been settled there.

But as a refugee, I had no choice about where I might be resettled. The way resettlement worked, at least from the perspective of someone living in the camp, was that a delegation from a particular country would arrive and word would spread through the camp where they had come from.

The French are here!

This time it's the Canadians!

After a few days, a list would be posted on a bulletin board outside the camp's main building. It listed the names of refugees who would be taken to that country. Those individuals would climb aboard motorized rickshaws and leave the camp, and the rest would continue waiting for their lucky time to arrive. Meanwhile, each day it seemed another boatload of refugees arrived, filling the already crowded camp with more and more people.

I heard these stories from other people during my first few days at the refugee camp. Many of them had already been living there, waiting, for several months. Thankfully, I had a very short experience in the camp, and I was extremely lucky. Less than one week after I arrived, a delegation from the United States showed up in the camp. Because I had only just turned 17 and was traveling alone without any relatives, the UN considered me an orphan. With this status, they granted me the highest priority in resettlement. The American delegation presented my first opportunity to apply, and sure enough, when the list of names appeared on the board, mine was among them.

When I read my name on that list, I wanted to scream with joy. Even though I knew nothing about the United States, and it was not my first choice, I felt so lucky to have been approved so quickly. After everything I had been through, I could hardly believe it. This moment felt like the culmination of my entire journey, the reason I had left my home and my family. Yet, when the moment arrived, I struggled to comprehend what it really meant. I had no idea what life in America might hold for me. I only knew that another journey lay ahead, more travel and another transition.

In the days after I learned I would be resettled in the United States, I received two letters: one from my older sister and one from my brother. Together, they had escaped from Vietnam and been resettled in Vancouver, British Columbia. In my sister's letter, she told me that I should do everything in my power to try to reach the United States. She felt that the Canadian education system was unfriendly to foreigners because it required English proficiency before entering school. By contrast, she had heard that the United States offered English as a Second Language (ESL) classes for refugees and other non-English-speaking students in public schools. Education was the key to survival in a new country, and so my sister urged me to go to the U.S., even if it meant living apart from my siblings.

Meanwhile, my brother held the opposite opinion. In his letter, he advised me to come to Canada so that our family could be reunited. I felt conflicted. I don't know if my siblings knew about their competing letters, but their words left me torn. I agreed with my brother that resettling in Canada would be better for our family. It would feel good to have someone waiting for me in the new country when I arrived. On the other hand, I had already accepted resettlement from the Americans. There was no indication if or when a Canadian delegation might arrive. If I gave up my spot, there was no guarantee I would be accepted by another country. I could end up spending many more months in the refugee camp. In the end, I decided not to say anything to the authorities about my brother and sister. I resolved to follow my sister's advice. More than anything, I was anxious just to get out of the refugee camp and be settled somewhere. So, I decided I would go to the United States.

At that point, I had only a small amount of money left, about $20 USD, which I tucked safely into my duffel bag. It wasn't much, but I had saved it all that time. Unsure of what the future held, I never knew when I might be hungry again.

***

On the day of our departure from the refugee camp, a convoy of rickshaws arrived. Local police assembled those of us chosen to leave and loaded us into the backs of the vehicles.

I held tightly to my duffel bag as I took my seat. Only about thirty refugees left with me that day, and I could not help but think about the thousands more still waiting for their turn. Men, women, and children gathered to watch our trucks depart. On their faces, I saw a mixture of despair and hope. Each and every person had a story like mine, one of sacrifice and perseverance. And like me, each one hoped for their own happy ending.

From the refugee camp, we drove back to the port through which I had arrived. There, we boarded a fishing boat which ferried us to Singapore.

If coming from the Indonesian island to Tanjung Pinang had been a shock, arriving in Singapore was a bolt of lightning. Unthinkably tall buildings loomed over us while cars and buses careened past on streets crowded by droves of people. I felt my head spinning as we once again transferred from boat to bus for the short drive to the Singapore airport. There, a specially chartered TWA jetliner waited on the tarmac. The entire plane was filled with Vietnamese refugees. I could hardly contain my excitement. I had never been on an airplane before. Scarcely had I imagined flying over the tops of buildings and trees, let alone crossing an entire ocean to another continent.

Soon I was on board the airplane, and we hurtled down the runway and lifted into the air. I was so excited, I kept trying to look over the people next to me and out the window. I wanted to explore everything. I ran my fingers over the seat, flipped through the magazine in the seat-pocket, opened the air vent and turned the light on and off. Below, I saw the streets and buildings of Singapore grow smaller and smaller until they appeared like toys. Then, we flew out over the ocean, and I saw the clusters of green and brown islands amid the vast sea of blue. It was hard to believe that just a few weeks ago, I had been living there on one of those secluded islands. Already, that time felt like a distant memory.

***

Our plane touched down at a military base in Oakland, California on the afternoon of September 15th, 1979, my first day in the United States. We stepped off the plane and were immediately shuffled through the process of receiving official immigration papers which recognized our status as refugees. I was surprised to see that the men processing our paperwork were also Vietnamese. I wondered if they were refugees themselves or somehow employed by the U.S. military as refugee processors. Of course, I didn't have the chance for small talk with them, but it was helpful to be greeted in this new country by people who spoke the same language. After the formal paperwork was taken care of, we loaded a bus bound for a hotel to spend our first night in America.

It may not seem extraordinary now, but stepping aboard that bus gave me my first taste of just how different life in America would be. The bus was similar to any you might see at a Greyhound station, but I had never been on something so luxurious! As I took one of the plush, cushioned seats, I felt a blast of cold air coming from a vent near the window. Air conditioning! I rubbed my hand over the soft seat covering and marveled at how new and clean everything appeared. My experience on buses in Vietnam bore no resemblance to this. Hard metal or plastic seats, dirty floors and grimy windows were common. Air conditioning consisted of a window you could crack to increase airflow.

I don't know why the bus had such a profound impact on me, but I truly felt like a boy who had discovered gold. It seemed emblematic of the new, luxurious beginning that lay before me. I would be treated like a prince, transported from one place to another in gleaming, climate-controlled vehicles. At that moment, I couldn't imagine that I would face any more challenges.

By this time, it was evening, and the sun had set. As we drove out of the military base and entered the Bay Area traffic, I once again found it hard to sit still. To reach our hotel, we had to cross what I now know is the San Francisco-Oakland Bay Bridge. Crossing the bridge that night, I was mesmerized by the sight of so many red taillights glowing ahead of us. To me, it looked like an endless red snake, curling its way across the dark expanse. I kept standing up in my seat to get a better look through the windshield at the shifting red lights. I knew what they were, just cars on the road, but I had never seen so many. I couldn't help myself. I was so excited to be in America that I wanted to soak in each and every detail.

After crossing the bridge, we pulled into the parking lot of a Travelodge hotel. The entire hotel had been booked to house refugees coming from Vietnam. Stepping off the bus, I heard a woman speaking in a language I could not understand. Suddenly, for the first time in the whole resettlement process, I realized I didn't speak a single word of English. Here I was in America, the country I had longed to reach, with absolutely no way to communicate. At that moment, my excitement dwindled. The realization struck me that, far from being over, a new phase of challenges had only begun. Despite America's comforts and conveniences, I had a lot to learn. My excitement remained, but for the first time, it was tinged with fear.

Some Vietnamese helpers showed me into the hotel and to a room with two queen-size beds. A young couple and their small daughter were already in the room. They greeted me and told me I would be sharing their room. Four people in a hotel room might seem like tight quarters, but after the cramped confines of the refugee camp, it felt spacious. In fact, the hotel room was not much smaller than the home I had shared in Saigon with my parents and six siblings!

The luxuries continued through the evening with the arrival of dinner. My first meal in the United States was Kentucky Fried Chicken with mashed potatoes and corn on the cob. What a decadent feast! This was the first time in my life that I had eaten so much meat. In Vietnam, we frequently ate chicken, but we would cut a breast or thigh into small pieces to share among the whole family. Now I had an entire breast and drumstick to myself! The crispy skin crunched with each bite, leaving my face and hands covered in greasy residue. It was wonderful! It tasted so good that after devouring my whole meal, I cleaned out the corners of the box, ensuring that no morsel of delicious chicken or potatoes was left behind. After surviving for so long on the meager scroungings of the island and basic staples in the refugee camp, my stomach felt like it might burst. But it felt so good to be truly full and satisfied for the first time in months.

***

I stayed for two days at the Travelodge hotel. We hadn't been told to stay inside, but I felt so intimidated by the outside world that I hardly set foot outside the hotel room. The hotel was on a busy thoroughfare, and from the window of my room, I could watch the cars speeding past. Even if I had wanted to leave, where would I go? I didn't speak the language, and everything seemed so foreign to me. The weight of my ignorance and vulnerability felt palpable. I had survived a week adrift at sea and months on a desolate island. I had used my strength and ingenuity to find and trade for food, to collect firewood and water. I had faced the death of a small boy before my eyes. But now I couldn't even gather the courage to cross the street.

Instead of venturing out, I stayed in the hotel room and watched TV. Everything was in English, so I couldn't understand much of what happened in the shows. I played with the remote control, a device I had never seen before. It seemed like some kind of magic wand, and I flipped through the channels with it until I found a cartoon featuring Bugs Bunny or Wile E. Coyote. These I could follow without the need for language.

After two days of watching cartoons, pacing the hotel room, and eating fried chicken and instant lo mein noodles, a Vietnamese woman arrived and informed me that it was time for me to meet my new foster parents. I confess this was another aspect of resettlement in America to which I had not given much thought. I was seventeen years old and had nearly finished high school in Vietnam. I had left my own family and been handed into the care of the three sisters and their families. But truthfully, I had begun to think of myself as independent. Enduring the boat and the island in the company of the three sisters felt like it had been more of a burden than a help. I wasn't sure I was ready to integrate into a new family once more.

But in the eyes of the U.S. government, I was a minor. That meant I had to be placed in foster care. Once more, I packed my few belongings and boarded another bus to the next uncertain phase of my journey.

6. Foster Family

In order to understand my experience in the United States foster care system, it's important to realize that I had no understanding of that system when I entered it. I had been told, from other children and families in Vietnam, that upon arrival in the United States, Vietnamese children were adopted by white families. In the rumors, these American families were wealthy, kind-hearted people who would take care of refugee children, send them to school, and make sure they succeeded in their new environment. Somehow, I also had gotten the idea that each family sponsored individual children, paying for them to resettle in the United States. And so, when I stepped on that Greyhound bus, on my way to meet my new foster parents, I believed I was meeting the very people who were directly responsible for my survival and escape from Vietnam.

Of course, this was not the case. I had no concept of the vast bureaucracy and state-sponsored nature of the foster care system. I was correct that many foster parents are good, kind-hearted people, but in no way could I have conceived that, far from having financed my journey to the U.S., my foster parents were actually *paid* a stipend from the government in order to house me.

With all these misconceptions in mind, I clutched my duffel bag—the same piece of luggage that had carried all my belongings since the day I left my parents' home in Saigon—and boarded a Greyhound bus bound for Sacramento. My heart pounded for the entire two-hour ride. The excitement was coupled with an intense fear. I truly had no idea what to expect.

When I stepped off the bus in Sacramento on September 17, 1979, I was met by two women—one Vietnamese and one white. The Vietnamese woman introduced herself as Tuyen Williams. I would come to learn that she had married an American G.I. and now worked for Catholic Social Services helping resettle Vietnamese refugees. Mrs. Williams indicated that the woman standing next to her was my new foster mother, Mrs. Debra Campbell.

***

Mrs. Campbell and I stood across from each other for a moment, sizing each other up. What I saw was an older woman—around sixty years old—with short white hair and a face that looked like it was set in pale plaster. She stood only about five feet, two inches but with a protruding belly. The most remarkable thing I noticed about her in that first glimpse was a dark brown cigarette smoldering between the fingers of her right hand. I had never met a woman who smoked.

I can't be sure what Mrs. Campbell was thinking in that moment, but I'm sure the boy who stood before her seemed just as foreign as she did to me. I was a scrawny, seventeen-year-old Asian boy clutching a worn-out, black duffel bag with a bewildered look on my face.

Tuyen Williams explained to me in Vietnamese that she worked for the Sacramento branch of Catholic Social Services and that I should not hesitate to let my new foster mother know if I ever needed anything. Mrs. Williams said she would always be available to help. I bowed my head respectfully, greeting Mrs. Campbell in the typical, polite Vietnamese way. And with that, Tuyen Williams left me alone with my new foster mother.

Mrs. Campbell gestured me to follow her and led me through the bus station parking lot to a blue, two-door, hatchback Honda Accord. I climbed into the passenger seat, and we drove wordlessly out of the city. I thought that I had been nervous before, but now a true terror began building inside me. Strange and unexpected as my journey had been up to that point, I had always at the very least been surrounded by people who shared a similar background and experience. My relationships with the three sisters, for example, had been strained, but at a minimum we could communicate with each other in the same language. Now, as we left the city of Sacramento behind, and the northern California countryside began to roll past the Honda's windows, I realized how isolated I was. I had just been placed at the mercy of this complete stranger.

Mrs. Campbell drove and drove. With no way to communicate, I sat silently in the passenger seat of her car, looking out the window. The landscape around us became more agricultural, and I recognized rice fields, not so different from those in the Vietnamese countryside. Finally, we turned into a long driveway between two fields and came to a stop in front of Mrs. Campbell's house. Before stepping out of the car, I looked around me. Green rice fields spread endlessly in every direction. We had passed a neighbor's house a few minutes before, maybe one mile away. Apart from that, we had truly arrived in the middle of nowhere.

***

The Campbells' property consisted of about ten acres. Beside the house sat two domed, metal Quonset huts. Between them, a dog cage held two enormous Dobermanns that barked ferociously as I approached the house. Some distance away was a small barn where chickens scratched in the dirt. A cow and several goats grazed in a pasture nearby. In another field were the largest birds I'd ever seen—emus, I soon learned—and a handful of peacocks.

Mrs. Campbell proceeded to give me the tour, gesturing and speaking to me in the inscrutable sound I knew was English. She led me into the first Quonset hut which was filled from floor to ceiling with bird cages. Exotic birds of all varieties squawked and chirped, and the sound reverberated off the sloped metal walls. Bins and barrels full of bird and dog food sat stacked around them. In the other Quonset hut were more cages and a kitchen which smelled strongly of dog food.

Mrs. Campbell led me inside the house and showed me to my bedroom. The space was small, with a twin-size bed pushed against one wall, but it was very clean and orderly. From this, I gathered that I would be expected to keep my room spotless and tidy. By American standards, the room was extremely modest. But it was the first time in my life that I had ever had my own private room. My whole life, I had slept on the floor, packed among my siblings like a sardine in a tin. A soft bed of my own felt strange and luxurious.

Falling asleep that first night, I thought of all the places I had lain my head over the past year: unfamiliar houses of relatives and strangers in Vietnam, the tarp-covered roof of a boat at sea, a burrow of sand beneath a bush on a remote island, a wooden bench in an Indonesian refugee camp, a hotel in San Francisco. And now, my own bed in a bizarre place I was expected to call home. I had arrived, finally, in the place that should have felt like a destination: America, with a white adoptive family. But somehow, I felt more unsettled than ever. For the first time in months, I was no longer on the move. No longer in transition. It seemed unreal that I now lived here in this world of barking dogs and squawking parrots. I felt some relief in knowing that surely I would soon be enrolled in school. I would be able to learn English and set myself on the course of my new life. With this consoling thought, I allowed myself to sink into sleep.

***

Over the next few days, I settled into something of a routine. Each morning I woke up, cleaned my bedroom and made my bed, ensuring that everything was as orderly as it had been when I first set foot in the room. Then, I set about completing the list of chores that Mrs. Campbell had given me.

Mrs. Campbell and I had discovered, after several hours of frustrating gesturing and shrugging, that she was from Louisiana and knew a bit of Cajun French. Paired with the French I had learned from my short time at the Catholic school in Vietnam, we were able to develop our own rudimentary pidgin language. In this way, I learned something about her life. She ran a cottage business raising and selling exotic birds and breeding small dogs as pets. She also bought large quantities of wholesale bird and dog food and resold it to her customers.

My primary responsibility in the house was the care and feeding of all these animals. Each morning, I refreshed the water in every birdcage, fed the cows, chickens, goats, dogs, and emus, then collected eggs. Every other day, I also completed the foul job of changing out the feces-covered newspaper which lined the bottom of all the birdcages. This work was tedious but not difficult. Compared to the demanding physical labor I had performed daily on the Indonesian islands, it was easy. Still, I began to wonder why I wasn't being sent to school. Was my entire life in America meant to consist of doing farm chores for an old white woman?

After a few days, I also met Mr. Campbell. In our broken language, Mrs. Campbell had mentioned her husband, but up to that point, it had just been the two of us in the house. That first Friday evening, a large, obese man came through the front door. He was over six-feet tall with a protruding belly and wore metal braces on his legs. Mr. Campbell, I learned later, had contracted polio as a child and now needed help to walk. With barely more than a hello to the strange new Asian boy in his house, this enormous man settled himself into an armchair in the living room.

I learned from Mrs. Campbell that her husband was an engineer who worked for GE in San Jose. Instead of commuting more than two hours each way, Mr. Campbell kept a trailer home in San Jose where he lived during the work week. Only on Fridays did he make the journey back to Sacramento. He stayed for two nights and left again Sunday evening.

Mr. Campbell was not unkind. He merely treated me with a detached disinterest. While home during the weekends, he spent most of his time in the barn, working on various construction and maintenance projects. Unlike Mrs. Campbell, we had no shared language, and he made little attempt to communicate with me. But Mr. Campbell was a big, gentle man. He made no demands or requests of me. While he was away during the week, I frequently forgot about him. And when he reappeared each Friday evening, he seemed neither surprised nor interested that I was there.

***

A short time into my stay at the Campbells' house, two events changed the dynamic of the household. First, another foster child arrived, a boy from Cambodia named Leng. One year younger than me, he seemed equally shy. But unlike me, Leng had grown up in the countryside and was very tall, muscular, and tan. Having been in the United States for a few weeks, it was interesting for me to watch the bewilderment on Leng's face as Mrs. Campbell gave him the same tour she had given me, showing him the dogs, the birds, the small yet private bedroom. His astonishment and fear displayed so obviously on his face. I wondered whether I had seemed so vulnerable and overwhelmed.

Like me, Leng spoke no English, but he also did not understand any French. So communication between him and Mrs. Campbell was even more difficult. However, perhaps because we had been through a similar experience, the boy and I could communicate relatively well using gestures and a handful of related words in Khmer and Vietnamese. Between the two of us, we developed a rotating schedule, dividing and sharing the household chores. On odd days, for example, he cleaned the birdcages while I fed the chickens and cows. And on even days, we switched. This system worked well for everyone, and Mrs. Campbell seemed especially pleased to have two hard-working Asian house servants.

The second disrupting event occurred a few days after Leng's arrival. One afternoon, a white social worker showed up at the house with a Cambodian man who served as a translator for Leng. The social worker met with Leng and me separately, always with Mrs. Campbell in the room. When it was my turn, the three of us—Mrs. Campbell, the social worker and me—all gathered in the dining room for what seemed like a very formal endeavor.

I wondered why there wasn't a Vietnamese translator as well. I understood almost nothing that the social worker said during that first visit, but with Mrs. Campbell interpreting into broken French, I learned that she was there for a routine check-in.

"Are you happy here?" the social worker asked through Mrs. Campbell. "Are you safe? Is there anything you need?"

At that time, I still believed that Mrs. Campbell's patronage was the only reason I had been allowed to come to the United States. I was hyper-aware that she was sitting beside me during the entire interview, relaying all my answers.

"Yes, of course," I answered. "I'm very grateful to Mr. and Mrs. Campbell for allowing me to stay with them."

My answer seemed to satisfy the social worker, and she began talking at length to Mrs. Campbell. Meanwhile, a question burned in my chest. I didn't want to appear presumptuous or unappreciative, but I had been there for over two weeks, and I felt like this was my only opportunity to reach out to someone who might be able to help me.

I waited for a lull in the conversation, and then, mustering all my courage, I managed to squeak out my question.

"When will I be able to go to school?" I asked.

Mrs. Campbell looked at me quizzically.

My heart thundered and my face flushed. I knew I had said something I shouldn't have. Mrs. Campbell turned again to talk to the social worker. I didn't know whether she had relayed my question or not.

After a few minutes, the adults stood up from their seats, and the social worker informed me that she would be back in a few weeks to check on me. I looked to Mrs. Campbell, but she avoided my eye contact. She shook hands with the two visitors, and before I knew it, they were out the door.

What had happened? Had Mrs. Campbell agreed to send me to school? In that moment, I was too shy and embarrassed to ask her directly. Instead, while Mrs. Campbell disappeared into the kitchen, I rushed to finish my chores, to show her that I was a diligent, hardworking person who was worthy of an education.

***

After the social worker's visit, I could hardly contain my excitement. I had taken a risk and I was sure it would pay off. Any day now, I would be allowed to start attending school. I would finally learn English and be on my way to becoming self-sufficient. One day soon, I would be able to leave behind the chores and monotony of the Campbells' house.

Sadly, as was the case with nearly every aspect of my journey since leaving Vietnam, my expectations did not match reality. Days passed, and then weeks, and there was no mention of school. I became so focused. I thought that if I just cleaned the birdcages a little more thoroughly, if I fed the cows and collected the chicken eggs a little more quickly, Mrs. Campbell would take notice and realize that I had done absolutely everything she had asked of me. Surely, she would reward me with the one thing I had asked for.

Two more weeks went by, and the social worker returned to the Campbells' house. Once again, she asked me about my care. Was I happy and safe? Once more, I told her yes, everything was fine. I reiterated how grateful I felt toward Mr. and Mrs. Campbell for their kindness in taking me in. And then, once more, I asked if I would be able to attend school.

Whatever excuse Mrs. Campbell gave the social worker for why I was not in school, it must have been convincing. The social worker again seemed satisfied that everything at the Campbells' house was normal. She stayed for a brief conversation and then left without incident. And again, I returned to the routine of daily chores.

I began to think that perhaps this *was* normal. I had heard stories of Vietnamese children going to the United States and becoming educated, but maybe they were just rumors. How was I to know what was "normal?"

After the social worker's second visit, when it seemed that once again nothing would change, that was the first time since arriving in the United States that I began to feel depressed. Until that point, through all the months of waiting, through the survival and perils of escaping Vietnam, my hope had buoyed me because I knew there was a goal to strive for—a new life in the United States. But now I had arrived, and my new life was nothing but the life of a servant. I spent those seemingly endless nights alone in my small room, lying on that soft mattress, staring up into the void of darkness above me, wondering if this was really all there was.

***

Perhaps Mrs. Campbell realized after the social worker's second visit that I would not give up on the idea of school. Or maybe the social worker pressured her to give in. Whatever the cause, shortly after that second visit, Mrs. Campbell finally told me that I would be starting school.

I was so elated. I thanked Mrs. Campbell profusely and once again redoubled my energy in completing my daily chores. I felt it was important to demonstrate that there would be plenty of time for me to go to school and still do everything around the house that was required of me.

As it turned out, time would not be an issue. The next week arrived, and I learned that the "school" Mrs. Campbell had promised me was a twice-weekly English language class, taught in the evenings at the local middle school. Monday and Wednesday nights, I would be allowed to attend the class, which lasted for one and a half hours each night.

Class was taught by an older white man who slowly led the group of students—most of whom were illiterate American adults or much older immigrants—through a series of lessons and exercises.

Immediately, it became clear to me that the pace of the class was mind-numbingly slow. The content itself was helpful—I learned the ABCs, basic pronunciation of words, and a few crucial English phrases—but if this was the only class I took, how would I ever be able to go to college and become a doctor?

I asked Mrs. Campbell if I could sign up for additional classes at the night school. She agreed to let me take a typing class that met for an additional hour on the same Monday and Wednesday evenings. My hope was that typing would help reinforce the words I learned in the English class. But it was very clear to me that this was not the type of school I had envisioned. I wanted to attend school full-time. I had nearly completed high school in Vietnam, but if I wanted to go to college in the United States, I knew that I had to attend an American high school.

Mrs. Campbell drove me to and from the night school in her blue Honda, and nearly every day, I asked her—first in French and then in my rudimentary English—when could I attend a *real* school? I could tell that this irritated her. Clearly, she had a vision of what an Asian foster child was good for—cleaning and housework—and I wanted to push against that mold.

***

As weeks went by, I began to feel extremely lonely. Each time we returned to the Campbell farm from night school, I felt the acres and acres of rice paddy fields insulating me from the outside world. I had not had any contact with a Vietnamese person since coming to live with the Campbells. There was no one I could talk to or share my frustrations with. Even Leng, the Cambodian foster boy, who could likely sympathize more than anyone, felt like a distant entity because we could not actually speak to one another. I felt isolated within my own mind, where my thoughts, trapped within my Vietnamese language, seemed quarantined, unable to escape.

I wanted desperately to talk to someone. I missed my family and friends in Vietnam. The last time I'd heard from my family was via telegram in the refugee camp in Indonesia. Even then, all I had learned were stilted facts. I knew that my brother and sister had survived their escape from Vietnam and had both been resettled in Vancouver, British Columbia. They knew I had been resettled in the United States but nothing about the reality of my daily life. I wanted to reach out and let someone know where I was and what was happening to me.

And so, I made a phone call. I had a slip of paper that I had carried with me since leaving Vietnam, sewn into the seam of my pants with my emergency money. On that paper was the phone number of a Vietnamese girl named Le Thi Lam, an older sister of the three children I had helped look after while surviving on the Indonesian island. I had been told she was a very good student and was excelling in the United States, attending college. She was living the dream I so desperately desired.

I knew that Mrs. Campbell would not allow me to call her. I had been forbidden from using the phone. But one day when she was outside, I dialed those numbers and listened to the faraway ring through the receiver. My hands shook as I listened to the tone. Each silence between rings felt eternal. I was sure she would not answer.

After several rings, I heard a click and a clear voice say in English, "Hello?"

"Hello," I said, answering with one of the few English words I had learned.

After a pause, she said a few more words in English that I did not understand.

I switched to Vietnamese. "This is Tiến Kim Lưu," I said, my voice quavering with adrenaline. "Is this Le Thi Lam? I knew your family."

Another moment of silence followed. I began explaining

to her that I had looked after her siblings on the island.

Finally, she answered in Vietnamese, "Thank you for helping my family. What can I do for you?"

I felt such relief at that moment. It felt so good to be talking to someone in my own language. My story began to pour out of me. I begged her to help me. To tell me how she had succeeded in attending school.

Le Thi Lam listened patiently. When I finished, she said that she had applied to community college and received financial aid with the help of her social worker. Ultimately, she was only a teenage refugee like me.

"I'm sorry," she said. "I wish I could help you, but I'm not sure what I could do."

My stomach sank. All the energy that had been coursing through my body suddenly drained. I realized how silly I must have sounded. What did I expect this woman to do? Drop everything in her life to come rescue me? She was right. There was nothing she or anyone else could do. Never had I felt more alone than in that moment. I thanked her for listening and slowly hung up the phone.

For a moment I stood there, stunned, staring at the silent phone. Calling my only Vietnamese connection had seemed like an emergency last resort. But it had accomplished nothing. Then I heard the thumping footsteps of Mrs. Campbell coming through the house.

I thought that I had made my phone call in secret, but Mrs. Campbell must have picked up another phone in the house during my call. Somehow, she found out that I had been using the phone. She was livid. She stomped into the room, screaming at me in English. Her face flushed bright red. Beads of sweat collected on her forehead. I backed away from the phone and cowered against a wall. I did not understand a single word of her screams, but the message was clear enough.

Mrs. Campbell picked up the phone I had just been using and dialed, seething as she waited for someone to answer. She spoke rapidly into the receiver and then held the phone out to me.

Unsure what was happening, I reluctantly accepted the phone and held it to my ear. On the other end, I heard the voice of Tuyen Williams, the Vietnamese woman who had met me at the bus station with Mrs. Campbell. She spoke to me in Vietnamese. "Mrs. Campbell has just told me that you've been disobeying her house rules. Is that true?"

It was all I could do to squeak out an affirmative sound.

"This is very serious," Mrs. Williams said. "We do not usually tell children this, but Mrs. Campbell has asked me to make it clear to you that during your first year in the United States, you are on probation. If you commit any crime or are found to be unsuitable for foster care, you could be sent back to Vietnam. Do you understand me?"

This information shocked me. I looked at Mrs. Campbell, who was standing next to me with her arms folded across her chest, glowering. I had never imagined this was a possibility, that I might actually be sent back to Vietnam. The prospect of returning, the shame and disappointment of my parents, the possibility of being drafted to fight the war against Cambodia, all of this terrified me.

"Do you understand?" Mrs. Williams said again.

"Yes," I said. "Yes, I understand."

I handed the phone back to Mrs. Campbell. While she and Mrs. Williams talked, I slunk out of the room, desperate to escape any remnant of Mrs. Campbell's wrath.

My cry for help had backfired. The futility of my position weighed on me like a heavy load across my shoulders. I thought about wading through the shallow channel of sea between the two Indonesian islands, carrying food and water for my survival. At least on the island there had been other people to help me, to commiserate with my experience. Now, there was no one.

***

After the incident with the phone call, my relationship with Mrs. Campbell continued to deteriorate. She no longer trusted me at all. She controlled my every movement and rarely let me out of her sight, except when I was at the night school class. She often made a point of telling me how expensive it was to house me—how much she spent on food and clothing. Not once did she ever mention that the government was providing this money to her. She allowed me to believe that I was a financial burden she bore out of the kindness of her heart.

Soon, the social worker made a third visit to the Campbells' house. With Mrs. Williams's threat fresh in my mind, I once again told the social worker that everything was fine. I made a point to mention that I was happy to be attending night school for English and typing classes.

The social worker left the Campbells' house without

incident. By this time, I had been living with the Campbells for nearly three months. But far from settling into a routine, I felt even more desperate and isolated than ever.

The mild temperatures of northern California's early fall had begun to cool and turn toward a wet, gray winter. The weather seemed to reflect the desperation of my mood. In the evenings, when my chores were finished, I often tried to steal a few minutes alone in the Campbell's barn. The sound of chickens clucking and scratching in the dirt mingled with the farther off cries of the exotic birds and the barking of the caged Dobermanns. Wearing an oversized sweatshirt that must have been a hand-me-down from Mr. Campbell, I lay on my back on a bale of hay, thinking about my future.

I thought about the nights I had lain awake on the roof of the boat, staring at the stars, dreaming of life in America. Now, instead of an education and a bright future, my life had descended into fear. Even in those few quiet moments, I was terrified that Mrs. Campbell would find me, accuse me of being lazy, and threaten to send me back to Vietnam. I could feel my nerves beginning to fray under the constant pressure of fear.

At the same time, I felt like something ever so slight had begun to change. Even though Le Thi Lam had told me she could not help me, just talking to someone honestly and in my own language had been an immense relief. Simply knowing that she had successfully navigated the system I felt so stuck in, and that she was now in college, gave me a small amount of hope. I was too terrified to risk making another phone call from the Campbells' house, but I wanted to talk with her again.

The following week, during a break between classes at the night school, I used a pay phone to call Le Thi Lam once more. The conversation went similarly. I pleaded with her for help, and once again she told me there was nothing she could do. However, she listened patiently and let me air my grievances. She was sympathetic to my feelings, and that alone was a comfort.

To this day, I don't know how Mrs. Campbell found out about that second phone call. While I was taking my English class, Mrs. Campbell took an upholstery class at the same night school. Maybe someone overheard me talking and told Mrs. Campbell. However she found out, when we got into her car after class that evening, she was even more furious than she had been before. For the entire drive home, she lectured me in French and English. She told me how ungrateful I was, how much she and Mr. Campbell had sacrificed to take care of me. I tried to apologize, but Mrs. Campbell would not be calmed.

In the past, when Mrs. Campbell had been angry with me, it had always passed fairly quickly. But this felt different. She only seemed to grow angrier as we drove closer to her house. I knew that I had crossed a line. In my mind, I had only been reaching out to a sympathetic ear. But to Mrs. Campbell, I had betrayed her trust completely. That moment felt like a breaking point. Afterward, nothing would be the same.

7. Fighting for an Education

The next morning, after Mrs. Campbell caught me using the pay phone at the night school, she drove me to Catholic Social Services to be confronted by Tuyen Williams. Mrs. Campbell led me through the door of the office where Mrs. Williams was waiting for me, looking stern, seated behind her long desk.

This was the moment I had been threatened with, I thought. This was when I would be deported back to Vietnam.

Mrs. Williams's voice was calm, and her outward demeanor remained pleasant, but I could tell that an anger equal to Mrs. Campbell's boiled beneath her skin.

"Tell me why you haven't been listening to your foster mother," Mrs. Williams said to me in Vietnamese. "The Campbells are your family now. You must obey them like your own parents. Otherwise, you won't be allowed to live with them."

Of course, Mrs. Williams didn't know me as a child in Vietnam. She assumed that I was a typical Vietnamese boy, stolid and obedient. If she had known the rambunctious hellion who had daily tested my mother's patience, she might not have made the same allusion.

Still, I did my best to show remorse and humility in that moment. I bowed my head silently as she reprimanded me for my behavior. Feeling truly terrified and depressed, I believed that Mrs. Williams was moments away from informing me that I would be sent back to Vietnam.

Mrs. Williams's mention of my family reminded me of my older brother and sister living in Vancouver, BC. Because I was an unaccompanied minor and had spent such a short time in the refugee camp in Indonesia, I had been accepted for resettlement in the United States before learning that my siblings were already in Vancouver. If the immigration authorities had known about older family members who had already been resettled, I likely would have been sent to live with them in Canada. But once I had been accepted to the United States, I hadn't mentioned my siblings. I didn't want to jeopardize the opportunity for higher education which I believed would be more achievable in America.

Now, at the moment when I believed I might be sent back to Vietnam, I decided to reveal my siblings in a last-ditch effort to save myself from deportation.

"What about my sister?" I said to Mrs. Williams. "Can I go live with her in Vancouver?"

"You have a sister in Vancouver?" Mrs. Williams seemed shocked that she had not been given this information before.

I reached into my pocket and pulled out the slip of paper which had my sister Luu Kim Thu's phone number written on it.

Mrs. Williams snatched the paper from my hands and dialed the number for my sister. Mrs. Williams, Mrs. Campbell, and I all waited in silence to see whether my sister would answer.

"Hello," Mrs. Williams finally said. She identified herself and asked the person on the other end of the line in English if she could speak to my sister. After another moment, Mrs. Williams switched to Vietnamese, and I knew that my sister's voice was now coming through the phone.

"I'm here with your brother," Mrs. Williams said. "Did you know he was here in the United States?"

I heard the low tones of my sister's response but could not make out the words.

"We would like to reunite the members of your family," Mrs. Williams said. "If you are prepared to have him live with you, Catholic Social Services will take care of all the costs and logistics of re-locating him."

She waited a few moments, listening, and then without saying a word, she handed the phone to me.

Warily, I held the phone to my ear. "Hello?" I said.

Immediately, my sister began reprimanding me, just as Mrs. Campbell and Mrs. Williams had done. "Our parents saved and sacrificed everything to allow us to escape Vietnam," my sister said. "What have you done for our family? You have been given the opportunity to live in the United States. It's your responsibility to get an education and *help* our family."

I could not find the words to respond. I was stunned.

"What have you done for our family?" my sister asked again.

"I—I don't know," I said. I began to cry.

"You cannot come live with me," my sister said. "It's much easier to go to school in the United States, and there are more opportunities. You must stay there so that you can become educated and help our family."

What could I say to my sister? Could I tell her, with Mrs. Williams and Mrs. Campbell sitting there beside me, that I was not allowed to attend school? That, after nearly three months in the United States, my only education was a night school class for adults? I was desperate to learn. The only thing I wanted since I'd left Vietnam was an education. I wanted to help our family. But what could I say? She was right. So far, I had done nothing.

I continued to cry silently, unable to form a response to my sister's rebukes.

"I will not allow you to come live with me," my sister said definitively.

With tears covering my cheeks, I handed the phone back across the desk to Mrs. Williams.

Mrs. Williams spoke to my sister for a few more minutes, but she could not be persuaded. I was not wanted in Canada with my siblings any more than I was wanted there in the United States with the Campbells. I was not wanted anywhere.

After she hung up the phone, Mrs. Williams translated the conversation for Mrs. Campbell who listened with a stone-faced expression. I continued to sob into my hands, unable to comprehend the words Mrs. Williams was saying but understanding everything about their meaning.

Mrs. Campbell stood to leave, and I started to follow her.

"No," Mrs. Williams said. "You stay."

I sank back into the chair across the desk from Mrs. Williams. I heard the door behind me open and then close. Mrs. Campbell was gone.

In that moment, the only thing I could imagine was that Mrs. Williams would now tell me that I was being deported. She would detail the process. The buses. The plane flight back to Indonesia. The boat to Saigon. I hung my head and tried not to make eye contact with her, as if that could delay my inevitable fate.

Mrs. Williams straightened papers and tidied a few things on her desk, letting the awkward silence build in the room. "Ok," she said finally. "Come with me."

I followed her through the Catholic Social Services building and out into the parking lot to her car. We got in, and she drove me to Rancho Cordova, a small city on the eastern outskirts of Sacramento where many Vietnamese immigrants and refugees lived. We parked in front of a dreary-looking apartment building.

Mrs. Williams turned off the car and turned to me. "You're going to stay here until we figure out what to do with you," she said.

I started to cry once more, feeling more abandoned and alone than I ever had before.

Mrs. Williams led me inside the building and unlocked a small, one-bedroom apartment. The place was unfurnished, and the empty rooms only contributed to the feeling of desolation that permeated the apartment. In the kitchen, a hot pot sat on the bare counter and a box of instant ramen noodles in one cupboard. Mrs. Williams brought in a sleeping bag from her car, which she unrolled on the floor of the bedroom.

With a few words of parting, promising that she would check in on me when she had figured out what to do next, Mrs. Williams departed, leaving me in the apartment alone.

***

For the next three days, I locked myself in that barren apartment, crying and feeling sorry for myself. Occasionally, I stared out the window, but the apartment was located deep inside a large complex. The only thing I could see from the window was the balcony of another apartment across a small courtyard. I watched people come and go, moving behind their curtains. I felt entirely separate from anyone around me, like an alien dropped onto a foreign planet. I didn't have a single penny to my name. I could barely speak more than a few words of English. I felt completely alone and helpless.

Several other Vietnamese families lived in the same apartment complex. They must have seen the terrified boy dragged in and left alone by the woman from Catholic Social Services or seen me looking forlornly out the window. Perhaps they had seen boys like me before. A couple of times during my stay, a neighbor knocked on my apartment door and invited me to have lunch or dinner with their family. I accepted, but I felt so depressed and scared that I could barely eat or converse with these kind neighbors. I knew that they, my countrymen and fellow refugees, could have understood my isolation and fear better than anyone. And yet, I felt so ashamed that I couldn't bring myself to tell them about my ordeal. I only smiled politely and accepted the bare minimum support they offered. After eating a quiet meal, I returned to my own apartment, where I stared out the window or lay on my sleeping bag, unable to sleep. I replayed my interactions with Mrs. Campbell and Mrs. Williams over and over in my mind. I didn't know what to do and I was terrified that I would be deported back to Vietnam.

On the fourth day, there came another knock at the door. When I opened it, I was surprised to see Mrs. Campbell standing in the hallway.

"I've agreed to take you home," she said to me in the matter-of-fact French we had grown accustomed to using with each other. "But only on the condition that you follow the rules. No phone calls. You'll do all your chores. And if you get mail, I will open it first to make sure you're not a communist spy."

I knew how difficult my life had been with the Campbells. I knew it was unlikely that she would send me to school. But I was so desperate and lonely, so anxious to get out of that terrible barren apartment, that I said yes. I followed Mrs. Campbell out to her little blue Honda which she had parked outside. Silently, we drove back through the city, out into those desolate rice fields, and to the Campbell farm.

***

After the experience of being left alone in that apartment, I became very quiet and withdrawn. My Cambodian foster brother and I silently went about completing the daily chores, and a sort of tenuous peace settled in the home. The social worker returned for another routine visit, and I told her yes, everything was fine.

Mrs. Campbell even began to loosen her grip on the household. She told the Cambodian boy and me that if we completed our chores, she would give us two or three dollars per week as allowance. Of course, we had nothing to spend this money on, living out in the country, but it felt comforting to save even those few meager dollars. At least if I was left alone again, I would be able to buy another box of ramen noodles when the first one ran out.

The most surprising change of all came soon after I returned to the Campbells' home. I don't know if Mrs. Williams or the other social worker finally convinced Mrs. Campbell to make concessions, but in mid-December of 1979, after three months living with my foster family, Mrs. Campbell finally agreed to send me to a real public high school.

One morning, she drove me about nine miles away to Grant High School so that I could take an equivalency test in English and math. The results would be used to determine which grade I should be placed in. Walking into that high school and sitting down for a test was an exhilarating experience. I felt so excited to finally prove what a dedicated student I was.

The math section of the test proved no trouble for me at all. I was highly fluent in the universal language of numbers and algebra. But when I got to the English section, I knew I was in trouble. I had only taken a handful of English classes at the night school. My typing lessons helped reinforce the few words I'd learned, but I understood almost nothing of English grammar, and reading comprehension at a high school level was well beyond my capabilities. I struggled through the test, making my best guesses at the meaning of passages and writing my answers in language fit for an English-speaking preschooler.

I felt exhausted as I finished the test but also happier than I had been in months. I realized how long it had been since I'd faced an academic challenge. It had been more than a year since my last day of school in Vietnam. My mind felt rusty, out of practice, but eager to learn again.

On the car ride home, Mrs. Campbell made a point of bringing up how expensive it was for her to send me to school.

"Public school is not free," she said. "Everyday Americans like me have to pay such high taxes so that you can go to school."

I knew that Mrs. Campbell was trying to make me feel guilty and indebted, but nothing could dampen the excitement I felt. Finally, I was going to school.

***

At the beginning of the next semester, January 1980, I began attending Norte Del Rio High School in Sacramento. Grant High School, where I had taken the placement test, was slightly closer to the Campbells' house, but because my score on the English test had been so low, I was sent to Norte Del Rio which had a dedicated English as a Second Language (ESL) program.

I remember waiting for the school bus that first morning. I stood at the end of the Campbells' driveway in the chilly

January air for what seemed like an eternity. Then I saw the bright yellow bus coming down the road toward me.

I stepped on board and immediately noticed that every other student on the bus was white. Strange, rapid-fire words I could not understand swirled around me as I took an open seat toward the front of the bus. The hissing of plural "s" words particularly caught my ear. In Vietnamese and French, plural words are not pronounced with an "s," so this sound always stood out.

On the bus radio, a song was playing. The tune sounded nice, but I couldn't understand a single word. By recognizing the tune, I later learned that the song was "Woman" by John Lennon. Even today, every time I hear that song, it brings me right back to that first morning of school in the United States.

The bus route was shared between Norte Del Rio and Grant High School. We stopped at Grant first, and all the white students got off the bus. We then continued to a poorer neighborhood of Sacramento where Norte Del Rio was located. As I walked into the building, I saw that the majority of students were Black or Hispanic. I definitely felt out of place as an Asian refugee, but at least I was not the only immigrant. In my ESL class, I met students from all over Latin America and a few others from Korea or other parts of Asia. We all shared similar struggles with learning the language, and the class was designed to help us not only learn the language but understand our class assignments so that we could do our best in school.

In addition to the ESL class that first semester, I had done well enough on the math placement test that I was allowed to take an algebra class with the general student population as well as a senior-level physics class. I did well in math, but physics proved a real challenge. The technical terms and dense language made reading the textbook nearly impossible. In class, when the teacher wrote out formulas and demonstrated concepts, I could follow along. But trying to study by myself with only a limited knowledge of English frustrated me.

All my life, my response to frustration had been to throw myself headlong into the challenge, and American high school was no exception. I immersed myself completely in those classes, especially ESL. I knew that the barrier to my success was not a lack of intelligence or dedication. Only learning English stood in the way of me getting a high school diploma and—hopefully—attending college.

English became my primary focus. In school in Vietnam, I had been so preoccupied with my standing among the other students. I always wanted to be at the top of the class and saw other students as my competition. But in America, I was so far behind that I barely noticed the other students in the high school. I focused on learning so intently that I spent all my time looking at textbooks and talking to my teachers. I didn't have time to make friends or compare myself to other students.

One teacher in particular had a strong influence on me during that first year in high school: my ESL teacher, Mrs. Sylvia Moran. Her parents had been born in Mexico and immigrated to the United States where she was born, so she had empathy for her immigrant students. She always went out of her way to make every student feel welcome and respected in her classroom. No matter where we came from or what our experience, Mrs. Moran dedicated herself to helping us master English so that we could understand our coursework.

I remember so clearly the book series we used in Mrs. Moran's class: *English for Today*. In addition to the rudiments of vocabulary and grammar, Mrs. Moran also taught us about American etiquette and customs, as well as clever phrases to help us navigate our daily lives. I zipped through those textbooks, devouring every bit of information that helped strengthen my English skills.

In addition to working with Mrs. Moran, I constantly practiced typing at home to reinforce my language skills. I also asked people to repeat phrases and words all the time. I'm sure that my enthusiasm was more than a little annoying, but my focus was so intense that I hardly noticed.

Attending high school that first semester felt like salvation, but life at the Campbells' house remained the same. I was still expected to complete all my household chores after school. Each day, Leng and I would divide the tasks. I would change the water for the birds and clean the cages while he fed the dogs and other animals. The next day, we would switch. Somehow though, the chores no longer felt like work.

I even began to enjoy learning a few things about farm life and raising animals. That spring, one of the emus laid an enormous egg and guarded it fiercely for several weeks until it began to hatch. I watched in amazement as the damp, alien creature pecked its way out of the shell and unfurled itself on the dirt floor of the barn.

Now that I was finally attending school, doing what I had been longing to do since leaving Vietnam, every new experience felt like an opportunity to learn. Each day, I did my chores cheerfully and then holed myself up in my bedroom to immerse myself in my lessons.

***

Even as I was enjoying my new foray into American education, I continued to face obstacles and challenges. One experience was especially painful. It is difficult for me to describe, yet I believe it's important to share so that others can learn from it and help prevent anything similar from happening to other vulnerable foster children.

As soon as I started attending high school, I began expressing to my teachers and Mrs. Campbell that my goal was to one day become a medical doctor. Often this information was met with skepticism or discouragement. Mrs. Campbell, in particular, impressed upon me how difficult and expensive it would be to attend college and medical school. But as usual, I was undeterred. I continued to talk about how much I wanted to study medicine.

One day, Mrs. Campbell told me she would take me to visit a friend of hers who was a medical doctor. I could talk with him about his experience and the path he took to become a physician. I could hardly contain my excitement. I didn't know what to expect, but I was eager to learn anything new that might help me in reaching my goal.

Mrs. Campbell and I drove through the suburbs of Sacramento and turned into a strip mall parking lot. It didn't look like the type of place that might house a medical office, but I couldn't be sure. I'd arrived in the United States just a few months earlier. How was I to know what the medical system looked like in this strange new country? I followed Mrs. Campbell into a storefront that appeared to sell potted house plants. No, this was definitely not a medical office. Still, I didn't know what to expect. Perhaps this was just a meeting place that Mrs. Campbell had arranged with her friend.

As we entered the store, Mrs. Campbell greeted a young white man, probably in his early thirties. He was clean-cut and professional-looking, and when Mrs. Campbell introduced me, he smiled warmly and shook my hand.

I was just beginning to understand and speak a few phrases in English, but the meaning of rapid-fire conversation was often lost on me. From what I could gather, Mrs. Campbell informed her friend of my interest in medicine and asked him to talk with me or show me something. I nodded my head politely, unsure of what to expect from this stranger. After a few minutes, Mrs. Campbell turned and walked out the door, leaving me alone with the man.

As soon as we were alone, the man gestured for me to follow him into the back of the store and said something about wanting to show me a device. Not knowing what else to do, I gave in to my curiosity and followed the man into a back room.

The room was sparse, almost like a medical exam room, though it still wasn't clear to me the nature of this man's business. He took a small black case out of a cupboard and set it on a counter. As I watched with interest, he opened the case to reveal a device that looked something like a flashlight.

The man pointed to his heart and then to his ears, explaining in slow English the purpose of the gadget. It was some kind of stethoscope, I realized, but not the type you normally see doctors wearing across their shoulders. This was an electronic device which when pressed against a patient's chest, would amplify the sound of their heartbeat.

The man unbuttoned my shirt and placed the stethoscope on my bare chest. Suddenly, I could hear the thumping of my own heart emanating from the device. I had never seen anything like this before, and I was excited to be learning something new.

As I was standing there, listening to the sound of my own heart, I felt the man's hands start to move from my chest down my torso. He was speaking to me, but I didn't understand the words he was saying, so I just continued to stand there. The man's hands moved methodically down my sides, across my belly and to my hips. He said something about showing me the way a doctor performed a physical exam.

Slowly, he unbuttoned my pants and pulled them down, working his hands down my legs and palpating my muscles. It was awkward, standing there in this unfamiliar place with this stranger's hands on me, but I didn't know what else to do. Mrs. Campbell had told me this man was a doctor, and so I trusted him. I stood stoically while he continued the exam. Then, gradually, the man worked his hands back up my legs and began touching my private parts.

I didn't know what to make of this. I was so naive. At seventeen years old, I knew almost nothing about human sexuality. My parents had been very strict about sex. They had never talked to me about the topic, and it was never covered in any of my education in Vietnam. I didn't even understand the process of puberty or secondary sexual characteristics for men and women. And I had never been exposed to any pornographic magazines or anything that might have helped me understand what this man had just begun doing to me.

As I stood there, frozen, the man started fondling my penis with his hands to the point where I became aroused. He continued for a few more moments until I ejaculated. I didn't know at all what to make of what had just happened. I admit that at the moment of climax, I felt a strong, pleasurable sensation. But nothing about the context felt right. I was so confused. But I didn't have any words to express myself, so I just stood there silently while the man retrieved a towel and wiped up. Then, without saying a word, he pulled my pants back up, I buttoned my shirt, and he walked me out to the front of the store where Mrs. Campbell was waiting for me.

I didn't understand what had just happened, but I didn't say anything to Mrs. Campbell. I knew that what the man had done to me was not right. Nothing about the encounter was consensual. What I now understand is this: a man saw a young boy in a vulnerable position, alone and unable to speak up for himself, and he took advantage of me.

I don't know whether Mrs. Campbell had any role in the abuse or had any idea what her friend had done to me. We never spoke about the incident. For years, I buried that episode deep inside myself. I locked it away and did my best not to let it affect me. When I thought about it, when I relived those details, it was extremely painful. Yet I knew intuitively that it was not my fault. I can't say that I was ashamed or embarrassed because I was so naive. More than anything, I felt confused. And so I didn't dwell on it. I didn't let it send me into a spiral of depression or anger. Instead, I tried to learn from it. I vowed never to allow myself to be put in a position like that again. And as I grew older, became a physician, and found myself in positions of authority with vulnerable people under my care, I promised to never let anything like that happen to anyone around me.

In the meantime, I returned to the Campbells' farm and to my studies. I remained focused on learning English and trying my hardest to succeed despite all the obstacles in my path.

***

I ended up doing well in all my classes that first semester. In fact, I progressed so quickly that at the end of my first semester, Mrs. Moran suggested that I should try enrolling in a regular high school English class the following year. I even managed a decent grade in physics despite my struggles with the dense language and terminology. But thrilled as I was by my success, I also felt an impending sense of dread as the end of the school year approached. Summer, I knew, meant a return to the Campbells' farm full-time, and two months without the escape and stimulation of high school.

8. Escape from the Farm

As the days grew warmer and longer, it became clear that Mrs. Campbell also did not want me hanging around the farm all summer with nothing but chores to keep me occupied. In the final weeks of the school year, she purchased two mopeds—one for me and one for Leng—so that we would not be confined to the farm. Next, she took me to a nearby Host International office where I filled out an application for a summer job at the Sacramento airport which was located just a few miles away from the Campbell farm.

One of the airport restaurants offered me a job as a pot and pan washer. I'd never done that kind of work before, but earning money and spending time away from the farm sounded like a good deal to me. I learned to ride the moped by practicing around the Campbells' property, and soon I could confidently navigate the dirt trails and roads between rice fields to get to and from the airport.

My days that summer consisted of chores around the farm in the morning—cleaning birdcages, feeding dogs, chickens and cows—and then, five days a week I would get on my moped and ride through the rice fields to the airport. I washed pots and pans in the airport restaurant for eight hours, usually from 3 to 11 p.m. Each night on my ride home, my moped's dim headlight illuminated the darkened rice fields. The warm air of the California summer rushed past me, and a sky full of bright stars burned overhead. They were the same stars, I realized, that I had gazed at from the tarp-covered roof of the boat on my journey from Vietnam. But here they were somewhat dimmer, filtered by the light pollution of the nearby city.

The cycle of chores, work, and sleep kept me busy and exhausted all summer. The work was strenuous. Some of the pots were large enough that I could have climbed inside and sat down. I had to lift and maneuver them into the giant washing sinks, sometimes enlisting the help of another kitchen worker. After one month, I started looking enviously at the dishwashers and busboys whose jobs seemed so much easier. But I was the new person in the kitchen, and my English wasn't good enough to work out in the dining room.

Still, there were many things I came to enjoy about my new job. For one, it gave me an opportunity to practice my English. The other restaurant employees consisted of people from many different backgrounds and ages. The kitchen was an aural soup of sizzling pans, steaming sinks, laughter, shouting, and conversation. The more time I spent around my co-workers, the more I began to understand them, and the more my speaking skills improved.

The other thing my dishwashing job afforded me was income. It wasn't much—I was paid the minimum wage of about three dollars per hour—but compared to the two or three dollars per week that Mrs. Campbell gave me for chores, I felt rich! I still had very little opportunity to spend my earnings, and so very quickly I saved up more money than I'd ever had in my entire life. My small stash of savings felt like a blanket of security, an insurance policy. I knew that if I was ever abandoned again, or found myself living on my own, at least I had money to feed myself and the ability to get a job.

***

Exhausted as I was by the pace of chores and work that summer, I developed a sense of freedom and independence I had not felt since leaving Vietnam. I was learning English. I was making money. I was looking forward to starting school again in the fall. For the first time, it seemed like I was on the path toward a new life in the United States.

But back at the Campbell house, not everyone was having as productive of a summer. The Campbells' other foster child, Leng, did not have a summer job. Perhaps he was too young or didn't have the correct paperwork. For whatever reason, when I left the farm every weekday afternoon, he stayed behind, confined to the property with nothing to do except the chores and projects Mrs. Campbell devised for him.

Like me, Leng saved his few dollars per week, but unlike me, he actually wanted to spend them. Having grown up in the countryside of Cambodia, he was a very athletic boy, tall and strong. And while academic pursuits were my focus, he prioritized physical fitness. Each morning and evening, he would do push-ups, sit-ups, and calisthenic exercises in his small bedroom. He often talked about how he wished he had a weight set so that he could better exercise his developing muscles.

Leng saved his allowance for several weeks, until he had about thirty dollars, and then he approached Mrs. Campbell and asked her to take him to Kmart so that he could buy a set of weights. But Mrs. Campbell, determined as she was to control our lives as much as possible, refused.

"You're not going to waste your money on that!" Mrs. Campbell said. "You'll use it once or twice, and then I'll be stuck with a useless set of weights."

Leng was typically as respectful and shy as me, but now he began to get upset. His face turned red, and he slammed his hand against the countertop in frustration. In his broken English, he said, "My money! I spend!"

But Mrs. Campbell could not be persuaded. The more he talked back to her, the more entrenched she became until they were shouting at each other in barely decipherable broken languages.

Then, as their shouts reached a crescendo, Mrs. Campbell lashed out and slapped Leng hard across the face.

Leng was physically strong and taller than Mrs. Campbell by several inches. He could have easily overpowered her and hurt her badly. But Mrs. Campbell's slap shocked him so much that he stood there, stunned, for a few moments before doing anything. Then, instead of fighting back physically, he turned and calmly returned to his bedroom.

A few days later, Leng and I were supposed to be outside helping Mr. Campbell expand the barn for the chickens and goats when Mrs. Campbell came asking for Leng. Mr. Campbell and I looked around and realized that he was nowhere to be seen. A quick search of the property revealed that his belongings were missing from his bedroom and his moped was gone.

Mrs. Campbell was furious. But she also seemed confident that he would return before long. After all, where could he go? We were surrounded by rice fields for miles in every direction, and the boy had no one to run to.

For several hours, she fumed and waited, pretending that she was going about her daily activities without concern. Finally, later that afternoon, Mrs. Campbell called the police and reported that her foster child had run away.

Throughout this whole ordeal, I remained a silent observer. I felt sorry for my foster brother, but I was also wary of bringing Mrs. Campbell's wrath upon me. I didn't want to sacrifice the newfound freedom I had recently gained. After Mrs. Campbell called the police, I got on my moped and went to work as usual. I was sure that when I returned home late that night, everyone would have cooled off and things would return to normal.

After my shift at the airport restaurant, I rode home with a feeling of trepidation in my gut. Had Mrs. Campbell found my foster brother? Had he returned on his own? What consequences would he face for being so defiant? As I rolled onto the property, I saw Mrs. Campbell's blue Honda Accord sitting in the driveway as usual. The lights in the house were dark, and there were no signs that anything was different from the way it had always been. But inside, the door to Leng's bedroom was open. His bed was empty. I had no idea where he had run away to, but it was clear he had not returned.

A few days later, the police, foster agency, and social workers discovered the truth. Apparently, Leng had also been making secret phone calls, though he'd been better at keeping them hidden from Mrs. Campbell. The Cambodian interpreter who had visited with the social worker had given Leng the phone number of a Cambodian refugee family that lived in Sacramento. After he left the Campbells' house on his moped, he had called this family from a payphone, and they had come and picked him up. He was now staying with this family and refused to return to the Campbells'.

Hearing this, I felt a mixture of relief and jealousy. I was happy that my Cambodian foster brother had managed to escape, and I hoped that the Cambodian family would treat him better. But I could not help feeling a twinge of sadness. Where was the Vietnamese family who would take me in? My attempts at calling other people for help had only landed me in trouble.

Of course, I didn't share any of these feelings with Mrs. Campbell. She had just lost half of her foster child labor force and the accompanying money she was paid by the state for our care. For days afterward, she acted even more sullen and irritable than usual. I did my best to avoid her wrath. I made sure to do my chores, along with those that Leng had been assigned, and concentrated on getting through the summer without another incident.

***

When school started again that fall, I was somewhat disappointed to leave my job at the airport, but I was also thrilled to return to the high school. I took a full course load that year. I enrolled in chemistry, regular 9th-grade English, 10th-grade biology, and an independent study advanced calculus course.

I quickly found that my English had improved significantly over the summer. I was able to follow lectures and assignments much more easily. Still, the English and biology classes were the most challenging. I remember being assigned to read *The Scarlet Letter* and not understanding it at all. Studying literature and writing alongside high school students who had been speaking the language their whole lives left me feeling slow. And reading a dense biology textbook full of complex terms and definitions was even more difficult. I was getting better, but my English skills still were not strong enough.

My teachers, however, recognized how much effort I put into class. They appreciated my hard work and often went out of their way to explain things to me or help me understand a particular lesson.

At home, I was so dedicated to my studies that Mrs. Campbell began to grow concerned. Every afternoon, I came home, completed my chores, and then holed up in my bedroom to study for the rest of the evening. She didn't think this was healthy, so she contacted the principal of my high school and told him she thought I should drop some of my classes in order to lighten my workload. I have to give a lot of credit to the teachers and administrators of that school because they did not give in to Mrs. Campbell. The principal told her I was doing well in my classes and that I seemed to enjoy them. He saw no reason at all for me to drop.

Mrs. Campbell did not like being told she was wrong. In her mind, she knew what was best for her foster children despite the fact that one had recently run away and refused to return.

Mrs. Campbell was never one to give up a fight easily. After being blocked on the academic front, she decided to focus her attention on my social life.

"You need to make friends," she told me. "You can't spend all your time alone in your bedroom."

This seemingly newfound concern for my emotional wellbeing took me by surprise, and I wasn't sure how to respond. Admittedly, I hadn't made any friends at the high school, but only because that was not my focus. I wanted to get a diploma and move on to college. In my mind, high school seemed temporary, a necessary steppingstone to the next, more important thing.

But Mrs. Campbell would not be dissuaded. She contacted my math teacher, Mr. Raymond Chayo, and told him that I was studying too much. She wanted him to help me make friends.

Mr. Chayo was a kind and dedicated teacher, so he took Mrs. Campbell's advice to heart. He organized a little party at his house and invited several of his math students. But as the day of the party approached, Mrs. Campbell got wind of who the other students were. Apparently, they did not fit her idea of who she wanted me to associate with. She told me they did not come from good families and that I needed to make better friends. In the end, she forbade me from attending the party.

Mrs. Campbell's decision did not sit well with Mr. Chayo. He had gone out of his way to do something she'd asked, and at the last minute, she'd backed out. Mr. Chayo could not understand it, but for me, it was only the latest in a long line of confusing and contradictory actions by Mrs. Campbell. Still, this seemed to mark a turning point. Years later, I learned that several of my teachers thought Mrs. Campbell was mistreating me, and they even talked among themselves about trying to find someone else to open their home to me. However, it wasn't until nearly forty years later that I learned the full truth of what happened next.

***

One day that fall, I was going about my afternoon chores when Mrs. Campbell called out to me from the house and told me to slaughter one of the chickens for dinner. I had never done that particular job before, but I had seen it done many times in Vietnam, and it seemed like a straightforward task. First, I found a large pot in the Quonset hut kitchen, filled it with water, and set it on the stove to boil. I knew that a crucial step was to scald the chicken in hot water prior to plucking its feathers. Then, I took a sharp knife and went down to the barn where the chickens lived.

I knew how to catch a chicken, how to approach it from behind and pin its wings to its body so that it couldn't flap away. I chose a chicken that looked large and healthy and then, like I'd seen men do so many times in Vietnam, I used the knife to make a quick slit across the chicken's throat. The chicken thrashed in my arms for a few moments as it bled, but soon stopped moving, and I carried it back to the kitchen where the water was now boiling steadily.

Holding the chicken by its legs, I carefully lowered it into the steaming pot of water. But the chicken must not have been completely dead, or else there were some lingering reflexes in its body, because as soon as it touched the water, its wings started flapping violently. Boiling water splashed up from the pot and doused my right forearm. I dropped the flailing chicken onto the floor and ran to the sink to put my arm under cold water.

Even as the cold water stopped the burning, I could see blisters forming on my scalded right forearm. The pain was so intense that I could not stand still. After a few minutes, I ran into the house to my bedroom, and for some reason, started typing furiously on my typewriter. Somehow, that repetitive action helped me cope with the searing pain.

Mrs. Campbell must have seen me run inside, or else she was wondering why her chicken dinner was delayed, because she arrived in my doorway moments later. After seeing my burn, she wrapped ice cubes in a kitchen towel and held them to my forearm to ease the burning. After a few minutes, even though the pain was still terrible, I had calmed down somewhat, and Mrs. Campbell convinced me to get up so that she could drive me to the hospital.

At the community hospital, the doctor diagnosed a second-degree burn. A nurse debrided the blisters, applied some burn cream to my skin and wrapped it loosely to cover the affected area. The cream helped soothe the most intense burning, but the pain lasted for several days.

What I learned nearly forty years later was that my ESL teacher, Sylvia Moran, saw the burns and bandages on my arm and thought they constituted child abuse. She brought it to the attention of the school principal, and together they filed a report with Social Services.

Once again, the diligent teachers and administrators at that high school proved to be my saviors. I didn't know at the time that they'd reported Mrs. Campbell, but not long after I burned my arm, I arrived home from school on a Friday afternoon to find Mr. Campbell home from San Jose for the weekend.

"Well, Paul," he said to me as I walked in the house. "Mom has decided to return you to the state. She thinks it will be best for you."

I was totally confused. Mrs. Campbell was nowhere to be seen, and I feared that I would be placed alone in the abandoned apartment again. Of course, I know now that Mr. Campbell was lying—or maybe he believed what Mrs. Campbell had told him. It was one last jab from the Campbells, whose expectations I could never seem to meet.

Trying not to think the worst, I went to my bedroom and hurriedly began packing my belongings. I looked for the sleeping bag that I had used at the Rancho Cordova apartment, but it was wet in the laundry. I was scared that I'd be left by myself once more without even a sleeping bag!

Within half an hour, a social worker was knocking at the

front door. Mr. Campbell stood aside stoically as I carried my small duffel bag past him. I didn't know where Mrs. Campbell was, but she never took the time to say goodbye to me. I followed the social worker to her car. Mr. Campbell closed his front door as we backed out of the driveway. As we turned onto the country road, I turned back one last time to watch the Campbells' farm, and all the pain it represented, disappear.

9. A New Family, A New Chance

After being removed from the Campbells' house, the social worker drove me directly to an emergency foster home. On the way there, she made it clear to me that this was a temporary placement for short-term crises. She expected me to behave and follow their rules but also to be ready for relocation in days or weeks.

The new foster home was about ten miles away from the Campbells in the town of Elverta. Like the Campbells' house, it felt like the middle of nowhere, but at least this house was in a neighborhood with other houses nearby.

The social worker walked me to the door of a small house—much smaller than the Campbells' large farmhouse. Her knock was answered by a kind-faced white woman who introduced herself as Lena Baumann. Mrs. Baumann took me inside and introduced me to her husband, Lyle.

The Baumanns lived a very simple life, especially compared to the chaos of the Campbell farm. The modest house sat on about an acre of land with a large, grassy backyard. At the back of the house was an enclosed porch with a pool table.

Already, it seemed more welcoming than the chorus of barking Dobermanns and squawking I'd been greeted by at the Campbells'.

The Baumanns had hosted foster placements before, which I learned when Mrs. Baumann led me to the bedroom I was meant to occupy. The walls were painted pink, and the room was decorated with dolls. The Baumanns' most recent foster child had been a little girl, and since I was only there as an emergency placement, they hadn't bothered to redecorate. But I didn't mind the décor. The room had a desk, and it was a quiet place where I could sleep and study. At that moment, that was all I wanted in the world.

While the Baumanns were an experienced foster family, I was the first Asian foster child or refugee they'd hosted. Immediately, they wanted to ask me questions about myself and my experience. This was something entirely new! The Campbells had not shown any interest in me, and I felt shy talking about myself. I told them a bit of my story, and they listened with curiosity and empathy. They also told me that Mr. Baumann worked as a machinist for the Northern Railroad, and Mrs. Baumann stayed home as a housewife. They didn't have much money, but I soon learned that they were extremely kind and generous with what little they had. It was such a relief to be in a welcoming home where I felt like a member of the family rather than a hired farm worker.

Of course, my main focus remained schoolwork. Now that I had moved even farther away, the school had to arrange a special bus to pick me up and drive me more than an hour to Norte Del Rio High School. News spread among my teachers that I'd been removed from the Campbells' house and was staying in an emergency foster home.

My teachers must have understood my dedication. I never would have been able to succeed in high school without their kindness and attention. They all recognized that the only thing I needed was a stable place to live so that I could concentrate on graduating and moving on to the next phase of my life. Luckily, the Baumanns ended up providing exactly that.

Initially, I was only supposed to stay with the Baumanns for a few weeks, but we got along so well that they asked my social worker to make the placement permanent. This was a huge relief to me. The Baumanns had given me my own small room in their house, and unlike Mrs. Campbell, they didn't expect any work from me in return. Still, I did my best to be helpful around the house. I went out of my way to help with cleaning, doing dishes, and generally making the house tidy. Mrs. Baumann was so impressed by this. She told me I was the first foster child they'd ever had who did those chores without being asked.

One day, I asked Mrs. Baumann if she would take me to Kmart to buy a tape recorder. I had come up with the idea of recording lectures at school so that I could listen to them again at home, stopping and starting at my own speed. I had also been working with one of the secretaries at the high school on my English pronunciation. She read chapters from my textbooks aloud to me, pausing at strange or difficult words and coaching me though their pronunciation and meaning. I thought that recording these sessions would allow me to listen and practice later.

Mrs. Baumann drove me to Kmart, and I picked out a tape recorder and started carrying it to the register to pay. But Mrs. Baumann stopped me.

"I can get that for you, Paul," she said.

I was so taken aback that I couldn't form the words to answer her. I had some money saved from my summer job washing pots and pans at the airport and was prepared to spend it.

Seeing my surprise, Mrs. Baumann explained, "The state gives us plenty of money for your room and board," she said. "It's part of being a foster parent, and there's often extra money left over."

I was stunned! During my whole time at my first foster placement, Mrs. Campbell had allowed me to believe I was nothing but a financial burden on her. Never had she offered to buy me anything beyond the bare necessities, and I had no idea she received any money from the state for my care. This revelation from Mrs. Baumann felt like an immense weight lifted from my shoulders. I still felt grateful to Mrs. Baumann and her husband for taking me in, but the sense of indebtedness and burden I'd felt at the Campbells' was suddenly gone.

Throughout the time I stayed with them, the Baumanns continued to host short-term foster placements. When each new child arrived, I did my best to help them feel at home and acclimated to the environment. They would stay for a matter of weeks or months before moving on to a permanent placement. The fact that out of all their foster children, the Baumanns chose me to stay made me feel valued and welcome in a way that I had not felt since coming to the United States.

***

While living with the Baumanns, I was also able to regain contact with my family. Long distance phone calls to Canada where my brother and sister had been resettled were expensive, so I didn't make many of those. But I was able to write letters to them and to my parents back in Vietnam, letting them know that I was safe in a new foster placement and that I was concentrating on my studies. I remember writing one letter in which I detailed some of my difficult experiences at the Campbells' house, but I did my best to minimize that trauma. I knew that from my family's perspective, I had been given a rare and valuable opportunity to be educated in America. That remained my sole focus.

Very soon, that renewed focus started to pay off. I began excelling in all my classes, even those that were most difficult for me, like English and biology. When the next semester came around, I enrolled in an independent study advanced calculus course and 10th-grade English. In addition, one of my science teachers suggested I take some science classes at the local community college.

At that time, I didn't understand the distinction between high school and community college. I didn't realize that I could take classes at the community college and receive credit toward a four-year university degree. I was also concerned that if I left high school, I might be cut off from the foster care system and all the supports that came with it. I remembered the trauma of being left alone in that bare apartment in Rancho

Cordova. I didn't know how I could support myself alone while attending school. But it was explained to me that as long as I continued living with the Baumanns, I could remain in the foster system until the age of 21, regardless of whether I was a high school or community college student. With these concerns addressed, I explored the option of taking classes at Sacramento City College. Ultimately, it turned out that the commute by bus to the college was too difficult. Because the Baumanns lived so far outside the city, the bus only came by once every two hours. I never ended up taking community college classes. Still, just knowing about all these options felt like a whole new world of opportunity.

Around the same time, I started thinking seriously about applying to four-year universities for the following year. Another Vietnamese student had graduated from Norte Del Rio the year prior, and he'd gone on to attend University of the Pacific (UOP) in Stockton, CA. I decided to apply there and to UC Davis, which was close enough to Sacramento that I could live at home with the Baumanns while attending.

My grades were good, even in my advanced classes, and I think this, along with glowing recommendation letters from my teachers, outweighed my difficulty with English in the application essays. That spring, I received letters of acceptance from both universities.

It was great news, but I faced a serious dilemma. University of the Pacific is a small private school which required all students to live in the dorms for their first two years. If I left the Baumanns' for Stockton, I would give up my status as a foster child and would be left on my own financially. UOP had offered me a generous scholarship, along with some loans and a work-study position. Theoretically, there would be enough money, but I was terrified that I would somehow fail academically. I had been told that university courses were much more challenging than high school. Without the support of my foster family, what would happen to me if I failed out? Would I end up living in a barren apartment in Rancho Cordova, working as a dishwasher? I worried that I would not be able to make it on my own.

UC Davis, on the other hand, had not yet processed my financial aid package. I didn't know how much support I would get from them, but it was a public university. And it was located close enough that I could live with the Baumanns while attending, keeping my foster child status and the support of a family that cared for me.

UOP seemed like the right choice, but I struggled to overcome my fear. Many nights I lay awake in bed, worrying that the language barrier and culture shock would be too much, and I would have to drop out. I turned the pros and cons over and over in my mind, agonizing over what seemed like the biggest decision of my life.

One day, as I was wrestling with my decision, Mrs. Baumann came to my bedroom and asked if she could talk to me.

"Paul, I know you're facing a big choice right now," she said. "I want you to know that whatever choice you make, any time you need a place to stay, you will always be welcome here."

Once again, with a simple word of kindness, Mrs. Baumann lifted an enormous weight from my chest. It had not occurred to me that the Baumanns would support me regardless of my official status as a foster child. Throughout my time in the U.S. foster care system, I had always felt like the housing and support I received was contingent—first upon labor and obedience, and then on state funding. The Baumanns, however, truly considered me a part of their family, a feeling that extended deeper than any official status and would last longer than any legally-mandated timeline. Finally, I felt free to make the choice I knew was the best one for my future. I made up my mind to attend University of the Pacific.

Unfortunately, there was still one more hurdle for me to cross before I could begin my college career. Since I had only been attending an American high school for a year and a half, I had nowhere near enough credits required for a high school diploma. That meant that before I could be officially accepted by UOP, I had to pass the GED test.

I was confident about my ability to pass the math and science sections but more than a little anxious about the English test. I had taken many tests throughout my academic career—both in Vietnam and the United States—but this was the most important test of my life. If I didn't pass, I wouldn't be able to pursue my dream of a college education.

On the day of the test, I woke up with a terrible cold. My nose was running, my eyes were red. I felt as if someone had stuffed my head full of dry cotton. Already I felt nervous. Now I had to battle my own body as well as the test!

Somehow, I managed to struggle through my cold and pass every section of the GED test, even the English portion. When I received my score in the mail a few weeks after the test, I felt so relieved. I had achieved the first major accomplishment on my American educational journey. I had survived high school and been accepted to a university. Now it was time for me to go off into the world on my own and pursue my dreams even further.

***

My first university experience ended up not being at UOP. That summer of 1981, I applied and was accepted to a six-week summer program at UC Davis for high school students interested in medicine or degrees in science. The program was sponsored by the National Science Foundation for "high achieving seniors interested in medicine and science." I felt honored to be chosen for it, since I never considered myself to be a top high school student.

During the program, students from all over the country came to UC Davis. They stayed for six weeks in the dorms and took classes from renowned professors at the university. Many recent high school graduates used it as a way to jump start their college career.

For me, the decision about whether to attend the summer program was more complicated. Students were required to stay in the UC Davis dorms for the duration of the six-week program. In the eyes of the foster care system, that would mean I was no longer living with my foster parents. If I attended the program, I would be officially cut off from the Baumanns, the foster care system, and all the supports that came with it. I would be truly on my own immediately after graduating from high school.

When I learned I was accepted, I stayed up late one night, sitting in my small bedroom at the Baumanns' house which had begun to feel like home, making a list of pros and cons. I'd already made the decision to attend UOP in the fall, but for some reason that still felt far away, whereas the summer program felt immediate. A host of fears swirled in my mind. Fear of the unknown, fear of failure, fear of being on my own. But Mrs. Baumann's words were also in my ears: *you will always be welcome here.* After hours of anxiety and deliberation, I made the decision to attend the UC Davis summer program. Once I'd made the decision, the fears turned to excitement, and I fell asleep dreaming of the new experiences that lay ahead of me.

Mrs. Baumann drove me to UC Davis on the first day of the program and helped me carry my bags of clothing and books into the dorm. I was so scared and intimidated by the other students arriving that day. Looking around, I knew that these were top American students from all over the country. During the six-week program, I met valedictorians, people who had scored a perfect SAT, and others who had been accepted to special pre-med programs at prestigious universities. Compared to them, I felt so insufficient. I hadn't even earned a high school diploma. I'd barely passed the GED test. How could I possibly hold my own with these geniuses?

However, once classes got started, I settled into a routine and was able to relax and enjoy the experience. I may not have had the impressive GPA and test scores that some students had, but I knew how to work harder than anyone. I stayed up late most nights, re-reading my notes from the day's lectures and reading the textbooks. During class, I was quiet and kept to myself. But I was attentive and studious. Knowing that I could succeed among this highly gifted group helped me feel more prepared and less nervous about attending UOP in the fall.

When Mrs. Baumann picked me up at the end of the summer, I was thrilled that I had survived the UC Davis program. I felt like there was nothing I couldn't accomplish. The summer program had provided me with something I'd been looking for since I arrived in the United States: a place to live on my own where I could dedicate myself to learning. The whole way home, I talked excitedly about all the new things I had learned and how anxious I was to start my freshman year of college.

After a couple of final weeks with the Baumanns, my foster parents helped me pack my few belongings and load them into their car. Mr. and Mrs. Baumann both drove the hour or so down to Stockton with me. I thought I was prepared, but the closer we got to the university, the more nervous I became. This was it. As soon as the Baumanns dropped me off, I would truly be on my own for the first time. I'd been given a small taste of college during the summer program, but I still felt self-conscious about my English skills and wondered whether I would really be able to withstand the academic rigors of an American university.

We turned onto Pacific Avenue in Stockton, and suddenly

the ivy-covered brick buildings of the campus came into view. Driving slowly onto campus, watching other students unloading their belongings and hugging their parents goodbye, everything felt like a dream. I could not believe this beautiful campus with its tree-lined greens and immaculate buildings would be my home for the next four years.

The Baumanns parked in front of Grace Covell Hall, the largest freshman dorm on campus, where I had been assigned to live. Across the street stood two large fraternity houses and two sororities with Greek letters above the doors. Together we carried my things into the building and into my dorm room— not unlike the small bedrooms I'd had in the Campbells' and Baumanns' houses. The Baumanns wished me the best and reiterated that any time I needed a place to stay, their home was always open.

After the Baumanns' departed, I was left alone in an empty room. For a brief moment, I flashed back to that empty apartment in Rancho Cordova where I'd been left by Tuyen Williams. Once more, I was on my own. That familiar fear and anxiety rushed in. But as soon as those feelings arrived, they were met by another emotion: excitement. This was not Rancho Cordova. I was not being abandoned to fend for myself in a cold, unfeeling world. Rather, I was being given an opportunity, one I had been striving toward since leaving my home in Saigon. I had made it to an American university. Now was my chance to become educated, to set myself on a journey toward a new, prosperous life. I began unpacking my clothes, books, and few possessions, settling into my new home. Once again, the journey ahead felt uncertain, but now I at least knew I was on the right path.

10. An American Education

For the most part, my college experience at University of the Pacific was tremendously positive. I made friends quickly with other students in my dorm. We went to the dining hall to eat meals together, and every Wednesday night we attended a free movie screening on campus. But apart from those activities, I mostly kept to myself and spent the majority of my time alone in my room, studying until midnight or later nearly every night.

From the very beginning of college, my focus was on medical school. The university library had a book which listed every medical school in the country, along with their requirements for enrollment. I spent so much time poring over that book that I practically memorized it. I learned, for example, that in order to be a competitive applicant for medical school, I needed to take a heavy schedule of math and science classes. I also reasoned that if I took science and math classes first, I could continue to practice my English skills so that I would be better prepared for more reading- and writing-heavy classes in the future. So, my first semester at UOP, I took 18 credits, all of them in math and science.

This was a extraordinarily difficult course load. Compared to most of my friends and dorm-mates, I had much more homework and studying to do. Of course, my workload was compounded by the fact that my English skills were still not great. I could handle most of my science classes fairly well, but biology proved to be a real challenge. So much of the course required memorization of the Latin names for plants, animals, bacteria, and more. Reading the dense textbook in English was difficult enough, but now it seemed half of the words were in another strange language!

To make it through biology, I resorted to what had worked for me in high school. I used my tape recorder to record lectures so that I could listen back to them at my own pace, and I asked a graduate student to let me record her saying the Latin names. With these recordings, I could practice pronunciation in the privacy of my own room, which allowed me to better comprehend the course material.

My diligence and hard work paid off. I did well in my classes, receiving an A or A-minus in every course that first semester—even biology! But because it took me so much more time to study, I developed a grueling schedule to keep up with my classmates. Every day I woke early in time for my 8 a.m. class. Because I was taking so many credits, I usually had class until about 5 p.m. Depending on the day, I sometimes had time in between classes for lunch or to find a quiet space to read and go over my notes from that day's lecture. After dinner, I returned to my dorm room and studied until late at night.

Even though my focus was on academics, I also realized that I needed to take care of my health. I knew that if I got sick and had to miss class, I would fall hopelessly behind. So, I also devoted time every day to exercise. I signed up for a PE class and played badminton with other students. Frequently, after a long day of class and studying, I was so full of anxious energy that I had trouble falling asleep. I would go for long jogs around campus at midnight or 1 a.m. until I wore myself out enough to fall asleep. Then, I would wake up the next morning and start the routine all over again.

During that first year of college, I did little other than study, eat, exercise, and go to the movie every Wednesday night. It sounds exhausting—and it was—but I also felt enormously happy and fulfilled. Going into college, I had been nervous that I wouldn't be able to succeed or keep up with my American classmates. But with enough hard work and dedication, I had proved to myself that success was possible.

***

Because I was so studious, my professors took note of how much effort I put into their classes. Just like in high school, my teachers in college often went out of their way to be helpful and mentor me. Of course, I also made friends with other students, but because I spent so much time studying, I never became very close with them. I had friends and friendly acquaintances, but my most memorable relationships from that time ended up being with faculty and staff.

One man who really helped me during those first years of college was Mr. Belz, an administrator in the financial aid office. Because of my status as a refugee and foster child, I had to check in with the financial aid office every 2-3 months to review the status of my aid package and loans. Mr. Belz always welcomed me in and took the time to carefully review my application, making sure I understood every aspect of it.

Mr. Belz was a white man born with achondroplasia, a form of dwarfism, and perhaps he took a special interest in me because he saw us both as outsiders trying to fit into a world designed for others. One day, I ran into him while walking across campus between classes. His face lit up when he saw me.

"Paul, do you have a minute?" Mr. Belz said.

I had just left class and was on my way to the library to study before my next class, but I didn't have anywhere urgent to be, so I stopped and said, "Hello, Mr. Belz."

"Sit with me for a minute," he said. "I've been thinking about you lately." He gestured to a park bench, and we sat down in the shade of a nearby pine tree.

"How have you been, Paul?" Mr. Belz said. "How are you liking UOP so far?"

I told him that I was enjoying my classes very much and that I was grateful for the financial aid his office had been able to offer me.

Mr. Belz waved his hand to dismiss my gratitude. "I'm curious about *you*," he said. "Tell me about your family. What do you hope to do after college?"

It was strange, I realized then, that everyone on campus knew I was a refugee—or at least assumed so because I was Vietnamese—but no one had ever asked to hear my story.

And so there, on that bench in the middle of campus, I began to tell Mr. Belz about my journey to the United States. I described fleeing Vietnam by boat, leaving my family behind, surviving on the Indonesian islands, and coming to America and living with the Campbells and the Baumanns. I confided in him that my goal was to become a medical doctor so that I could help others and fulfill the promise I had made to the Compassionate Buddha. It was the first time I'd shared the whole story in that way.

As I talked, Mr. Belz sat quietly and listened, asking a few questions as I stumbled in my retelling. When I was finished, he nodded his head thoughtfully. "I believe you will become a doctor," he said. "And you'll make a very fine one."

Mr. Belz then shared with me his own hopes for the future. He was several years away from retirement, but already he was planning. He wanted to move to Europe, he said, to experience another culture and live in a new land. Together, the two of us sat and talked about the uncertainty and excitement that our future lives might bring.

We talked for so long that I lost track of time. When I finally looked down at my watch, I realized I was almost late for my next class. I apologized to Mr. Belz and said that I hoped we could continue the conversation another time.

"Of course, Paul," he said. "Hope to run into you again soon."

With that, I hurried off to class. I did run into Mr. Belz again, and he became a good friend and mentor to me during my time at UOP. In addition to helping me stay on track with all my financial aid paperwork, he encouraged me to pursue my dream of becoming a doctor. Without the support of Mr. Belz and others like him, I would not have been able to make it through the difficult times which lay ahead.

***

The first two years of college went by very quickly and, for the most part, smoothly. My classes were difficult, and the work was challenging. But I pressed ahead, not allowing anything to distract me from my studies. And University of the Pacific truly became my home during those years. During holiday breaks when the other students left campus, I stayed behind. The Baumanns always made a point of reaching out to me and letting me know that I was welcome to return to Sacramento and join them for Thanksgiving or Christmas. But holidays were difficult for me. Seeing everyone gather with their families to celebrate reminded me of my own family and the painful memory of leaving them. I didn't know what to do with these feelings, so I avoided them. I made excuses to the Baumanns and said I needed to stay on campus to study.

I remember one Thanksgiving during my second year at UOP. Everyone had left campus, and I was the only student staying in the entire dorm building. All those empty rooms around me felt like an enormous void. It seemed like the manifestation of all my isolation and loneliness. But rather than dwell on those feelings of sadness, I just immersed myself in work, studying the requirements of medical school and practicing for the MCAT entrance exam.

Also during my second year at UOP, I wrote letters to my sister and parents, telling them that I had decided to apply for medical school. Their response was not what I had hoped for. No one in my family had ever finished college. My parents had high hopes for their children, but my goal seemed too lofty. My mother and sister both suggested that I choose a career that didn't require so much additional schooling. I could be an engineer, or even a dentist, they said, with much less work.

My family's response was difficult to hear, but it didn't distract me from my goal. At that point, my mind had already been made up. I'd worked so hard already to get to that point. More hard work, no matter how difficult it might be, would not deter me.

During summer breaks, UOP also allowed me to stay on campus. But since classes were not in session, there was little studying for me to do. So, I enrolled in additional courses at the local community college and took work-study jobs on campus. I worked at the library, helping shelve and organize books, and in the international student office as a typist, helping process visa applications and other paperwork.

In short, I did everything possible during those first two years of college to stay busy. In doing so, I blocked out all my feelings related to my family, my experiences as a refugee, and my difficulties with my first foster parents. I didn't deal with my frustrations about the culture shock and my ongoing struggles with the language barrier. I thought that if I just stayed focused on my schoolwork, I didn't need to confront my emotions. But all the stress, loneliness, financial pressure, uncertainty about the future, and fear suddenly came crashing down on me during my third year of college.

My dream, of course, was to go to medical school and become a doctor. And junior year of college was incredibly important for that goal. It's the time when I needed to begin gathering letters of recommendation, essays, and transcripts and take the all-important MCAT exam. All this stress and my repressed emotions began weighing on me until I was on the verge of a nervous breakdown.

Suddenly, I began having difficulty concentrating while studying. Every time I opened a textbook, my head would spin, and my vision would blur with tears. I tried my best just to power through the way I had in the past, but even when I managed to read a chapter, I found that I couldn't retain any of the information.

My grades on exams began to suffer, which only added more anxiety and stress. I feared that finally I would be found out as the fraud I felt I was. I would have to drop out of college and never realize my dreams. Instead of studying, I started spending long hours curled up under a blanket in my bed, hiding from the world.

I stopped exercising. I no longer enjoyed going to the movies or eating meals with friends. I spent more and more time alone, consumed by depression and fear. Soon, my emotional distress began to show physically. I started looking pale and depressed. One day, one of my classmates, a woman named Rudene Dicarlo, recognized something was wrong and approached me.

"Paul, you don't look well," she said. "Is everything OK?"

I admitted to her that I'd been feeling depressed and unable to concentrate on my studies. Instead of dismissing my concerns, which would have been so easy to do, Rudene recognized how serious my condition had become and took the time to talk with me.

"Whatever you do," she said, "please don't do anything foolish. You're a very bright student and a good person. I know you'll be an excellent physician and an outstanding father someday. So don't do anything foolish."

I felt a small sense of relief hearing such kindness from one of my classmates. Rudene later went on to become a pediatrician, which was no surprise to me given how compassionate she was. She encouraged me to go to the student health center and seek treatment. Initially, I was embarrassed to do so. In Vietnam, talking to a counselor was a totally foreign concept. It felt like if I sought help, I would be admitting that I couldn't handle the stress of college. But I also knew that something had to change or I would not be able to continue my education.

So, a few days later I went to the student health center on campus and met with a psychologist. She helped me talk through my feelings and start addressing all the stress and fear I had been keeping inside myself. After that initial meeting, I started going to therapy sessions once per week at the student health center. These counseling sessions, along with the support of my friends like Rudene and mentors like Mr. Belz, helped me put my experience and emotions in perspective.

Already, I had overcome incredible odds to escape Vietnam, make it to the United States, and enroll in college. Meanwhile, there were millions of Vietnamese people still living under an oppressive communist regime. When compared with their struggles, my fears about not getting good grades or being accepted to medical school seemed so insignificant. I also started coming to terms with the emotional trauma I had suffered as a refugee and foster child. Talking about my experiences and feelings helped lighten the weight of them. And slowly, I began to emerge from my depression. I started being able to concentrate while studying, began enjoying time with my friends again, and started doing better in my classes.

I feel so fortunate that I had the help I did during that dark time. I was lucky to be surrounded by friends and mentors who noticed the warning signs of depression and took action. Only once, during my deepest period of isolation and sadness, did the idea of suicide cross my mind. It was not a serious consideration for me, but I could clearly see how it would have been easy to fall down that fatal path of despair. Luckily, University of the Pacific was such a supportive environment, and they had a fantastic, free student health center that allowed me to get professional guidance and support. My friends and my counselor helped me get my life back on track, and for that I am forever grateful.

***

In the spring of 1984, my junior year at UOP, I received word from my sister that my parents had been approved to immigrate to Canada to live with her. This was a momentous occasion for our family, and it also raised the possibility that I could visit them all in Vancouver for a reunion. But there remained one hurdle: the cost of a plane ticket. While at UOP, I subsisted off my scholarship funds and the small amount of money I earned from my summer jobs on campus. I had nowhere near enough money for a plane ticket to Vancouver. Luckily, my sister had held a variety of jobs by now and was more financially stable. She volunteered to send me $300 to pay for the flight to Vancouver. So, shortly after my parents' arrival that spring, I took my first airplane flight since the one that had brought me to the United States.

When I arrived in Vancouver, my parents, brother, and sister were waiting there at the airport to meet me. My body flooded with a complex mix of emotions. I hadn't seen my parents or siblings in more than five years. And yet, Vietnamese culture does not encourage displays of emotion, especially among men. As I approached my parents, we did not embrace or kiss. They did not tell me how much they loved me or missed me. My mother held out her hand to me, and I held it in mine. A few tears fell silently down her cheek. That was the extent of the emotion at our long-awaited reunion.

The next few days turned into a somewhat awkward visit. I'd spent so much time and mental energy learning English that I sometimes struggled to find the right Vietnamese word. I stumbled through strained conversations with my family, filling them in on the details of my ordeal that couldn't fit into a letter. And all the while, I was concerned with getting back to UOP. I worried that even a few days away would make my grades suffer or cause me to fall behind in my studying for the MCAT. I had changed so much that I felt as if a wall had been built between my family and me during our five years apart.

I returned to UOP with a sense of relief that I could refocus on my studies. I began compiling all the necessary elements for my applications to medical school. I took the MCAT and received a decent score. I solicited letters of recommendation from professors who I knew had recognized my hard work and dedication to my goals. But there was one element of the application that gave me tremendous anxiety: the essay.

Looking back now, my ambition astounds me. I had only been in the United States for a little over three years. My English skills were functional enough for daily life and to get by (with lots of help) in my math and science classes. But I still struggled massively with expressing myself clearly in writing. I knew that if I was going to write a coherent med school admissions essay, I would need a lot of help.

At that time, I had a work-study job as a typist in the international student office. I had always enjoyed typing, and even though my writing skills were lacking, I could quickly and accurately type visa applications and other official documents for my job. One of the secretaries in that office was named Sidney Hickey. During my hours there, she helped me learn how to correctly format and type things like formal letterheads, envelopes, and applications. Of course, this was back in the days before personal computers. All my typing was done on typewriters!

So, after I wrote the first draft of my essay for medical school, I asked Sidney to review it with me to help proofread and format everything correctly. Like so many others, Sidney was incredibly patient and helpful. She knew I was a refugee, and after we got to know each other, she sometimes invited me to her house for weekend and holiday meals. Once, when she moved from one house to another, she found a pair of sandals that no one in her family had used and gave them to me. This may seem like a small gesture, but I had so little money at that time—living off financial aid and student loans—that I could never afford new clothes. A pair of new sandals was quite a generous treat.

With Sidney's help, I drafted what I thought was a decent application essay and sent it off with my letters of recommendation, test scores, and transcripts. Knowing how competitive medical schools were, I sent my application to as many schools as I could, all over the country. Application fees were expensive, but my status as an unaccompanied refugee with essentially no income allowed me to apply for fee waivers for most applications.

Medical school applications required several rounds. If my preliminary application was accepted based on test scores, essays, and transcripts, the school would send me a letter requesting additional materials and essay responses for a secondary application. So, for the next few months, I received a handful of rejection letters along with a few requests for secondary applications. However, once I passed the secondary application, I ran into a roadblock. Once a secondary application was accepted, the school invited candidates for an in-person interview.

When I received my first interview invitation—from Northwestern University in Chicago—I quickly realized that

I had a big problem. First, I had already spent the money my family had given me on a plane ticket to Vancouver. I didn't have enough for another ticket to Chicago. And secondly, even if I managed to get myself to Northwestern, I didn't have any professional clothes to wear.

Once again, my friends proved to be my salvation. There was another Vietnamese student at UOP named Nguyen Thi Kim Loan. She was a pre-dental school student who came from a wealthy family. She knew that I was poor and needed clothes for my med school interviews. So, one day she took me to Macy's in the Sherwood Mall near the UOP campus. She helped me pick out a sport coat and bought it for me as a gift. It was yet another display of generosity that helped me get one step closer to my goal of becoming a doctor.

But that still left the issue of the plane ticket. I didn't have enough savings to cover the flight, so I reached out to my sister once more to ask for help. Again, she agreed to help, and she sent me the money to buy another plane ticket, this time from California to Chicago. I knew that I couldn't keep asking my sister for money indefinitely, but Northwestern was one of the best medical schools in the country, so I figured it was worth the expense, even if it meant that I wouldn't have the money to fly anywhere else. If I needed to interview elsewhere, I would figure it out when the time came.

So, in November of 1984, the fall of my senior year at UOP, I took my first trip in America outside of California. I flew to Chicago and arrived late in the evening. Since I didn't have the money for a hotel, I had arranged to stay in the dorms with a current medical student. I boarded the bus from the airport and drove along Lakeshore Blvd, watching the lights of the city on one side and the dark expanse of Lake Michigan on the other. I remember being shocked at how cold Chicago was. Coming from Vietnam and California, I had never experienced a true midwestern winter!

The next morning, I had my interview on the Northwestern campus. I met with several professors and current students, and everything seemed to go fairly well. I felt nervous and a bit out of place wearing my new Macy's sport coat, but everyone was very kind and welcoming.

After the interview, I flew back to California to wait for a reply. I truly didn't know what to expect. I knew that Northwestern was an incredibly selective medical school, but I thought I might have a chance since I'd already made it through two rounds of applications. Then, just a few days before Christmas break, I received a fat envelope with a letter inside saying that I had been accepted to Northwestern University Medical School!

I could hardly believe my eyes as I read and re-read the letter. All my hard work had finally paid off. I was going to be a doctor! It was the best Christmas present I could have ever asked for. Immediately, I called and wrote letters to everyone I could think of who had helped me get to this point: my student advisor, pre-med advisor, professors, parents, siblings, friends, and foster parents. I wanted everyone to share in my happiness. So many people had been generous with their time, money, expertise, and guidance. It felt like a miracle to be holding that acceptance letter. But it was a miracle created by dedication, hard work, and a lot of help along the way.

11. Becoming a Doctor

When I received my acceptance letter from Northwestern, I could have withdrawn my other medical school applications and committed to attending. But I had put so much work into preparing each application that it seemed wasteful to do so. Knowing that I had already been accepted to one school, though, helped relieve the immense pressure I had felt about applying and interviewing to such competitive programs.

Over the next several weeks, I had a few more medical school interviews. Luckily for my bank account, I was able to schedule them all regionally, so I didn't have to buy another expensive plane ticket. Instead, I took the bus to Los Angeles to interview at the University of Southern California. I also had an interview with Harvard, scheduled with a representative in Southern California. But the interview I remember the most vividly was at the University of California, Los Angeles.

Initially, UCLA was not high on my list of medical schools—though looking back, I'm not sure why. UCLA ranked in the top ten medical schools in the country, and it wouldn't require moving across the country to a frigid city like Chicago. Whatever the reason, I had not done much research on UCLA, but had applied almost as an afterthought. When I passed their preliminary application and received an invitation for an interview, I agreed, not knowing what would come of it.

It would have been easier and more convenient to fly from Stockton to Los Angeles, but once again, I did not have the money. So, I booked a ticket on an overnight Greyhound bus, which also saved me from having to pay for a hotel room. I tried my best to get a little sleep on the ride south and arrived at the downtown Los Angeles Greyhound station around 5:00 a.m. In the public bathroom, I brushed my teeth and then used a payphone to call the local bus operator to find out which route would take me to UCLA.

To my surprise, UCLA was located on the outskirts of the city, and the operator told me it would take nearly two hours to get there! Luckily, I had plenty of time. My interview was scheduled to begin at 9:00 a.m. that morning. So, I boarded the bus, which took me to another station, where I transferred to a second bus to UCLA.

When I arrived on campus, I felt overwhelmed by the enormous size. UCLA was like a city in itself! I longed for the small, comfortable environment of UOP that I had come to know so well. I asked some students for directions to the medical school and made my way across campus. In the medical school building, I found a bathroom, got dressed in my suit and tie, combed my hair, and then checked in at the student affairs office for my interview.

It had been a long and somewhat exhausting journey, but once the interview began, I settled into the routine and felt quite comfortable. Over the course of the day, I met with a medical student and three professors, all of whom seemed incredibly welcoming and warm. The final interview went particularly well. The professor was an emergency room physician, and for some reason, we really clicked. He seemed to like me and was impressed by my background and experience at UOP.

As the interview was coming to an end, the professor said, "Paul, if you do end up moving to LA and need a place to stay, please contact me and let me know."

I thanked him and shook his hand, grateful that I had made a personal connection.

As much as I would have liked to linger on campus and talk to the friendly faculty and students, I had to get back to the bus station for my return ticket that evening. After the final interview, I looked at my bus schedule and saw that the bus back downtown was arriving in five minutes! I ran across campus and arrived at the bus stop just as the bus was pulling in.

I hopped on board and settled into a seat, catching my breath and thinking back on my experience that day. UCLA had impressed me. Their students and faculty had gone out of their way to make me feel welcome. And with the ER doctor's parting words, I felt like I had a good chance of being accepted. I started to think that staying in California for medical school might not be such a bad idea.

The two-hour bus ride back to the Greyhound station gave me plenty of time to consider these options. Once there, I waited for the overnight bus back to Stockton.

When I arrived back at UOP the following morning, I had to go directly back to class and work. I had a position as a chemistry TA that semester, and I remember being so exhausted conducting lab work that afternoon. It had been a long forty-eight hours without much sleep. But even though interviewing for medical schools was tiring and expensive, I felt a sense of excitement knowing that the following year I would take the next big step toward my dream of becoming a doctor.

***

About a month later, I received a letter saying that I'd been accepted to the University of California, Los Angeles Medical School. Suddenly Northwestern, which I had been so excited about just a short time ago, no longer seemed like such an attractive option. I thought about the cold wind blowing off Lake Michigan and the darkness of that northern winter compared to the warm, sun-drenched campus of UCLA. Plus, Northwestern was a private institution, whereas UCLA was a public university. Being a California resident meant that staying within the state would make medical school significantly less expensive for me.

So, after two acceptances, I decided to withdraw my other applications. I didn't want any more expensive and tiring interviews. I also notified Northwestern that I would not be attending and officially accepted UCLA's offer.

Along with my acceptance to medical school came another financial aid application. I worked with Mr. Belz in the UOP financial aid office to complete the application and sent it in, hoping that I would receive some help. When my financial aid offer came back a few weeks later, I was stunned! UCLA had awarded me a four-year Regents scholarship, which meant my full tuition was paid as long as I kept good academic standing. If I had any doubts that I had made the right decision between Northwestern and UCLA, now they dissipated completely. I still needed to take out some federal student loans to cover room and board, but the Regents scholarship meant that I could attend medical school with significantly less financial strain.

Looking back on my time at UOP as graduation neared, I felt a sense of profound gratitude. In those four short years, I had grown up so much. Of course, I had also worked hard. I had gone into my freshman year with a sense of determination that I would make it through and be accepted to medical school. I thought about all the nights I'd stayed up late studying or memorizing the medical school requirements from that library book. But along the way I'd had so much help and guidance. My friends and mentors had been there to support me through one of the darkest periods of my life when I felt like I might not be able to go on. My professors and advisors had helped me stay on track in my classes and made sure that I was set up for success in medical school. I had made good friends and learned more than I ever thought possible.

In short, I realized how lucky I was that I'd attended a small, private school like UOP. If I'd attended a large university like UC Davis or UC Berkeley as an undergraduate, I might have been lost in the sea of students. But the small class sizes at UOP allowed me to form close relationships with professors and advisors. I hadn't recognized it going into college, but now, on my way out, I understood how fortunate I was to have made University of the Pacific my home for the past four years. Looking back now, I can say that my time in college was one of the best periods of my adult life, and certainly a time that changed me forever.

But now it was time to leave that comfortable environment and forge ahead once more into unknown territory. Those familiar nerves and self-doubt returned. Would I be able to keep up in medical school? Would UCLA feel as comfortable and welcoming as UOP had? Would I be able to survive if I had another nervous breakdown? All these questions fluttered around my head as I prepared to move to Los Angeles. But I did my best to push them aside and focus on my goal. I had already come this far. Now it was time to become a doctor.

***

During my final weeks at UOP, I started making plans for moving to Los Angeles. Once again, I took the overnight bus to LA to look for a place to live. Through all four years of undergrad, I had lived in the dorms on campus. This was my first experience trying to find an apartment on my own. I didn't have a car to drive around looking for places to rent, so I just went to campus, found a bulletin board by the student affairs office, and started calling phone numbers that had listed apartments for rent near campus.

I was shocked when I learned how much an apartment in Los Angeles cost! My room and board had been included in my financial aid package at UOP, and I had been paying about $150 per month for my shared two-bedroom apartment. The first few one-bedroom and studio apartments I inquired about cost close to $2,000 per month! There was no way I could afford that. Disheartened, I kept scanning the bulletin board and found a handwritten flyer that another student had posted. He was a first-year medical student looking for a roommate. I wrote down his number, walked to the payphone, and gave him a call.

The other student was in a similar situation, looking for an inexpensive place to live near campus. So, together we rented a one-bedroom apartment about a 15-minute walk from the medical school. The rent was $1,600 per month, $800 per person to share a bedroom with another student! Keep in mind, this was the mid-1980s. It seemed like an enormous expense, but it was better than trying to afford a place on my own.

I took the return bus back to UOP and finished up my last few weeks of class, walked across the graduation stage, and received my Bachelor's degree. Then, I packed up my books and clothes into a single suitcase and once again purchased a bus ticket—one-way this time—and moved to Los Angeles to begin my medical school education.

I was excited, but also worried that I wouldn't be able to handle medical school. At times, I wondered whether my acceptance to medical school was based solely on affirmative action rather than my own merit. I realized that my application stood out because of my experience as a refugee and "boat person." I had worked hard in high school and college, but I always felt academically inferior to my classmates.

The feeling was similar to the way I'd felt after the UC Davis summer program before starting college at UOP. I had succeeded initially—first high school and then college—but now I would be among an even more elite group of students. Medical school applicants, I knew, had to be among the top of their class from elite colleges all across the country. Already, I had almost collapsed under the workload and stress during college. Would I be able to withstand the increased pressure of medical school? I had learned some good coping skills from my counselor at UOP, but now I would be without the network of friends and mentors I'd accumulated in college. These anxieties grew within me as the first day of medical school approached. But my dream was more powerful than my fear. I resolved to push ahead and do the best I could.

**

During the first few weeks of classes, my fears were largely confirmed. Medical school was extremely difficult, and the rate at which we covered material was blistering. That first semester, I struggled the most with my anatomy class. Just like biology in high school and college, anatomy required so much memorization and pronunciation of strange-sounding body parts. Bones, muscles, ligaments; everything seemed to jumble together into an incomprehensible soup of foreign words. To get through the class, I did what I had always done: I studied as hard as I could.

Every night, I stayed up until 1 or 2 a.m., reading my textbooks, going over lecture notes, and practicing the pronunciation of medical terminology. My English skills had improved dramatically, but still I'd only been in the United States for a handful of years. I knew that I spoke with a heavy accent and still had difficulty understanding sometimes when people spoke quickly or used specialized vocabulary that I was only just beginning to learn.

Compared to the other students in my med school class, I felt so inadequate and intimidated. For example, my roommate had a photographic memory. It was scary! He only studied for one or two hours per day and still managed to be at the very top of our anatomy class. He came from an entire family of academics. His father had come to the United States from Australia to pursue a PhD in math and now taught at Cal State Northridge. My roommate had two brothers, one of whom was studying history at UCLA and the other at Harvard on a full scholarship.

Meanwhile, there I was, the first in my family to pursue an advanced degree, in a country where just a few years earlier I'd struggled to learn my first English phrases. I had to put in so many hours of study, cramming until two in the morning before every test. And still, I barely managed to pass. I felt out of place among my brilliant classmates. Everything seemed so easy for them that I sometimes wondered if I belonged there at all.

The pressure to succeed was intense. In medical school, if you failed one or two classes, you had to repeat the entire year. Plus, if I didn't maintain a decent GPA, my Regents scholarship would be revoked. Quite a few times during that first semester, I went to the student affairs office and asked whether any of my professors had complained about my academic performance. That's how worried I was that I would fail.

But somehow, after countless hours of studying and worrying, I managed to pass all my classes that semester. I was nowhere near the top of my class, though. At best, I was considered a mediocre student. This was quite a rude awakening for me. School in the United States had always been challenging, but until that point, I had been able to work harder and study longer than my peers and still reach the top of the class. Now, it seemed no matter how much I studied, I'd never be able to catch up to my genius classmates.

Eventually, I came to accept that I would only ever be an average medical school student. Still, I worked as hard as I could, but I tried not to compare myself with my classmates. Instead, I focused on learning what I could and treating my patients with compassion. If I couldn't be an outstanding student, at least I hoped I would become a great doctor.

With such a difficult schedule of classes and studying, there was no time for me to have a job or work-study position. I lived entirely on my financial aid and the small monthly stipend that came with the Regents scholarship. Without that aid, I never would have been able to afford medical school, even though a public institution like UCLA was comparatively cheap. I don't know what would have happened to me if I'd gone to Northwestern instead.

***

As I survived my first few semesters at UCLA, I started to think about what kind of medicine I might want to practice once I became a doctor. During the first week of classes, specialists from different medical fields gave lectures on their areas of expertise. I listened intently to each speaker, but as soon as the plastic surgeon started talking, I knew I'd found the field for me. The surgeon showed slides of some of his cases: hand surgeries, cleft palate and lip repairs, and reconstructions after injuries. I don't know exactly what about plastic surgery attracted me, but I felt a calling similar to the one I'd felt toward becoming a doctor after helping my fellow refugees on the boat.

I thought back to the games of dexterity and quickness I invented with my cousins in the back of my parents' store. I remembered my skill in foosball and badminton. All my life I've had excellent hand-eye coordination, so surgery seemed like a natural fit. And the range of cases and the ability to help people recover from disfiguring and debilitating conditions immediately drew me to plastic surgery.

So, beginning in my second year, I started setting up all my available elective courses toward the field of surgery. However, surgery was an even more difficult and competitive field than other specialties. I studied and worked as hard as possible, but classes continued to get more and more challenging.

After two years of medical school, I began doing clinical rotations, which comprise the majority of the final two years. In a clinical rotation, med students shadow doctors in various specialties and work directly with patients to gain hands-on experience. It's during this time that most students really discover what type of medicine they will practice in their career. By that time, I had already made up my mind that I wanted to be a plastic surgeon. I was told by my advisors, professors, and other students that if I was serious about pursuing surgery, it was crucial that I get an A in my surgical rotation.

During that 12-week rotation, I worked harder than I ever had in my life. I did everything I could to get that A. I asked questions of the physicians and residents I was shadowing. I took copious notes. I stayed up late every night studying and going over each case I had seen that day. I was particularly worried about the written exam at the end of the rotation. As usual, I felt self-conscious about my English and writing abilities. I studied as hard as I possibly could for that exam. Still, after all that effort, when the grades were posted at the end of the rotation, I received a B. I was devastated.

I remember talking to the secretary in charge of scheduling surgical rotations. She knew I wanted to be a surgeon, and when she saw the grade I received, she told me straight to my face, "Paul, you didn't get an A. You should consider going into another field."

Her bluntness shocked me, and I didn't know how to respond. My ego really took a hit, and I started to feel depressed that I wouldn't be able to achieve my dream. I wondered if she was right. Maybe I should reconsider my path.

After the incident with the secretary, I sought out one of the doctors from my rotation, Dr. Malcolm Lesavoy, who was a plastic surgeon. He had taken me under his wing after learning that I wanted to enter the same field, and I trusted his advice. I told him about the grade I'd received.

"Do you think it's still possible for me to be a surgeon?" I asked.

Dr. Lesavoy looked thoughtfully at me for a moment and then said, "Paul, we need more doctors like you in this field. Not just people who are good at taking tests, but doctors who are dedicated and love what they do."

His sentiment heartened me a bit, but I still felt depressed and wondered more than ever if I had chosen the right vocation. Still, there was nothing for me to do but press on. I had additional rotations to worry about, and they were equally challenging.

That same year—my third year of medical school—I had to do a six-week OB-GYN rotation at UCLA and Harbor-UCLA Medical Centers. It was not my favorite placement, but once again, I worked hard and thought I could do well enough to pass. However, after the first couple of weeks, I started clashing with one of the OB-GYN surgical residents. He was a white, male doctor who seemed to look down on me whenever I spoke up. Perhaps he didn't like my accent or could tell that I had to work harder just to keep up with the other students. Whatever the reason, he gave me a very bad review on my performance.

Then, at the end of the rotation, I had to take an oral exam at Harbor-UCLA Medical Center. During the exam, residents and attending physicians asked pointed questions about specific patients and cases we'd seen over the course of the rotation. One doctor—I remember she was a Chinese woman who had a reputation as a tough professor—asked me a question I didn't know the answer to. I did my best to stumble through a response, but even as I was giving it, I knew from the look on her face that it was wrong. It was no surprise to me that when the grades came back for that rotation, not only had I not done well, but I actually *failed*.

I was absolutely devastated. I didn't know what would happen. I thought I might get kicked out of medical school or at the very least lose my scholarship, which was dependent on maintaining good academic standing. After receiving my grade, I went directly to the student affairs office and asked them what would happen to me.

The woman at the student affairs office could tell I was distressed. "It's ok," she said. "You can use an elective credit to repeat that rotation. As long as you pass on the second try and you maintain your other grades, your scholarship won't be affected, and you can still graduate on time."

I was so relieved to hear that. I couldn't even imagine what I would have done if I hadn't been able to continue with medical school. Just thinking about all the work I had put into my studies made my head swim.

This failure set my progress back a bit. I had to do another six-week OB-GYN rotation. But this time, I was placed only at Harbor UCLA, rather than the UCLA Medical Center. I managed to avoid the tough professor who had challenged me during my oral exam, and I got along much better with the attending physicians and residents this time. At last, I was able to pass the rotation with no problems.

In terms of my overall studies, failing one rotation did not have too much of a negative effect. But psychologically, the impact was enormous. Already I had been struggling to find my place among my fellow students. Now, I felt like I was barely hanging on to my spot among them. I developed a constant feeling of nervousness and depression. Worried that I might suffer another nervous breakdown, I sought help.

At Harbor UCLA, there was a Vietnamese psychiatrist. I started meeting with him regularly to talk through my anxieties and fears. Having a shared first language and background helped me connect with him. The psychiatrist was a young man like me, doing his residency at UCLA. I told him about failing the first OB-GYN rotation and my constant fear that I would fail out of medical school. He listened empathetically, and talking to him gave me some perspective on my anxiety. I'd already come so far and accomplished so much in a short time. Regular therapy helped me overcome some of my nervousness and remain focused on doing my best in my remaining medical school rotations.

With this help, I did well in my fourth year of medical school and graduated on time with the rest of my class. I may not have been the brightest or most talented student, but I worked harder than anyone. Finally, I had achieved another major milestone on my journey. I was now a medical doctor!

Those four years of medical school were not as formative or positive for me as my undergrad years at UOP, but they were a necessary step, something I overcame rather than enjoyed. Earning my MD felt like a significant accomplishment. But already, I knew I wanted to be a plastic surgeon, which meant my medical training was far from over.

12. Residency and Medical Training

During my fourth year of medical school, I began applying for surgical residency programs. My ultimate goal was to become a plastic surgeon, which I knew meant first a residency in general surgery, followed by a fellowship or specialized residency in plastic surgery. Even though I had achieved my long-awaited goal of becoming a doctor, I still had many years of training ahead of me before I could enter practice as a fully licensed surgeon.

My grades in medical school had not been outstanding. And although I had a few mentors who helped me along the way, I hadn't made the type of strong connections I did during my undergrad years. Because of this, my letters of recommendation were not particularly strong. Still, I knew that a surgical residency was the only path forward, so I applied and hoped for the best.

There are two types of surgical residencies offered by medical schools and teaching hospitals: categorical residencies and preliminary residencies. Categorical residencies generally last five years and offer full medical board certification upon successful completion. These are the positions I and every other aspiring surgeon hoped for. By contrast, a preliminary residency is just that, an introductory training lasting up to three years which then requires re-application to an advanced specialty and additional training before becoming board certified.

Because the competition was so stiff and my performance in medical school had only been average, I knew that landing a categorical residency was unlikely. Sure enough, when the acceptance letters came back, I was offered only a three-year preliminary residency at Harbor-UCLA Medical Center in Torrance, CA, the same public hospital where I had done my second OB-GYN rotation. This news came as a bit of a disappointment because I knew it meant a longer road toward my ultimate goal. But I was also happy to have been accepted at all. I swallowed my pride and prepared for the next phase of my medical training.

***

As a resident, I became an extremely hard-working young doctor. I wanted to learn as much as I could and try every new skill. I paid careful attention to the more experienced doctors and nurses, making notes about the way they changed dressings, stitched and made incisions, and interacted with patients. Each evening, I was one of the last residents to leave the hospital, frequently staying until eight or nine in the evening.

For the first time, I was earning a modest salary. I no longer relied solely on scholarships and grants. I moved out of my shared student apartment and into my own one-bedroom apartment in Torrance, close to the hospital. At home in the evenings, I read textbooks and studied the latest information on procedures and surgeries I had observed that week. Each day at the hospital, I saw my patients, changed dressings, helped with surgeries, and went about my daily routine. I got along particularly well with the nurses at Harbor UCLA, which is important for any doctor. They appreciated my attention to patients and willingness to learn. I never ascribed, as so many young surgeons do, to the hospital hierarchy of doctors at the top and nurses and everyone else below.

In fact, I was a passive and timid resident in general. Compared to my colleagues, most of whom were typical surgical residents—aggressive and hyperconfident—I remained quiet and subdued. I knew my limits. I was not the most experienced or confident. But I also knew my strengths. In the operating room, my dexterity was excellent, and I went out of my way to treat the whole patient, checking in with them from the moment they arrived at the hospital until the moment they were discharged.

In general, I felt happy and successful. I was glad to be learning the skills of surgery and working toward my dream of one day becoming a plastic surgeon. But I also worked extremely hard. And at times I felt down or overwhelmed with work. Because I kept so busy, I didn't have time for much of a social life. Sometimes I felt lonely, missing my family in Vancouver and the sense of community I had forged during my years at University of the Pacific. At the same time, I was glad to finally have my own place, not to be dependent on anyone else for my livelihood. Long distance phone calls to Canada were expensive, but I called my family regularly to check in and update them on my progress as a surgical resident. However, just like when I'd visited them in college, our conversations were often strained. I began to realize that I'd become very "Americanized" in my ways of thinking and my attitude toward life. I valued my independence and own experience more than the advice of my parents or siblings. I often grew annoyed with my family, especially my mother, who constantly worried about me and asked each time we talked, "Did you eat yet?" I knew she was only showing her compassion and concern, but I became irritated easily, and often I would cut the conversations short, saying I had work or studying to get back to.

And it was true, my residency schedule was demanding. Each morning, I arrived at the hospital around 6:00 a.m. to conduct rounds on my patients, collecting all the information about any changes that had happened overnight. I then met with the resident team and chief resident to go over patient data and make decisions for their care. By 7:30, I would begin my work for the day, attending to patient care and observing or assisting in surgery. The days were long, and residents like me did not leave until the work for the day was done, often not until 8:00 or 9:00 p.m.

On weekends, the days were generally shorter. I might not have to be at the hospital until 7:00 a.m. and sometimes had afternoons off if there were no scheduled surgeries. But I also had to be "on call" once every three days. During on call days, I would stay at the hospital for 24 hours, responding to any urgent situations that came up. Often, this meant a long, sleepless night, and then I was expected to report to work the next morning as usual.

he only somewhat social activity I enjoyed was exercise. Two to three times per week, I would play badminton or volleyball with some of the other residents. But for the most part, I slept, ate, and worked.

The work was incredibly demanding and stressful, but by this time, I had developed tools for dealing with psychological and emotional stress. During my residency, I kept regular appointments with a counselor at the hospital to make sure I never became too overwhelmed and incapacitated the way I once had during college. For three years, I worked and learned as much as I could, never forgetting my ultimate goal of becoming a plastic surgeon.

At the end of each year of the preliminary surgical residency, we had to take written "in-service" exams. This was the most stressful part of the whole experience for me. As usual, I studied frantically, staying up late every night in the days and weeks leading up to the exam. Each time, I barely passed the tests. I did just well enough to stay in the program.

Normally—especially in a categorial residency—if you don't perform well on your exams for two years in a row, the program will transfer you to a lab for a year to do research and catch up on academic performance before returning to surgery. I'm sure that would have been my fate if I had been accepted to a categorical program. But because my residency was only preliminary, they allowed me to continue with general surgery.

Looking back now, it's amazing to realize how mediocre

my performance was in medical school and residency. I never scored high on the in-service exams. I never stood out among the residents when answering attending physicians' questions. If I had relied on my talent and skills alone, I likely would have failed out many times over. But I took what abilities I had and paired them with dedication and work ethic. Undoubtedly, there were many doctors who were smarter and more gifted than me. These factors were out of my control. The only factor I could control throughout my medical training was to make sure that no one worked harder than I did.

I also realized that I could focus my energy on my patients and caring for them as best I could. I often spent more time than my resident colleagues sitting with patients, talking with them about their lives outside of the hospital and listening to complaints that might not be listed in their charts. This patient-centered approach sometimes allowed me to see things other doctors may have missed.

One example came during my first year as a resident at Harbor-UCLA Medical Center. Even as a surgical resident, much of your first year is spent caring for non-surgical patients, doing whatever work is needed in the hospital and learning how to be a better doctor. One day, a Vietnamese man was admitted with a high fever. The man was also HIV-positive, but his disease had not progressed to the point that it constituted AIDS. The doctors were stumped as to what was causing his fever. He didn't appear to have an infection or respiratory disease like the flu.

I sat with the man and talked to him, something none of the other doctors had taken the time to do. Of course, the fact that I spoke Vietnamese helped. I learned that he'd recently returned from a trip to Vietnam. Suddenly, it clicked. The man was presenting with classic symptoms of malaria—a disease that was incredibly rare to see in California, but very common in Asia. I ordered a test, and sure enough, it confirmed my suspicion. We were able to quicky get the man on the correct prescription to kill the malaria parasite, and he made a full recovery.

Because of this experience and others like it, my attending physician at Harbor-UCLA Medical Center suggested that I consider switching to internal medicine, to focus on primary care rather than a specialty like plastic surgery. But as I continued through my surgical residency, I found that my attention to bedside manner and listening to patients helped me as a surgeon as well. I was able to notice small problems in pre- and post-operative care that other surgeons might have missed. I may not have had the academic accolades that some of my colleagues did, but I knew that I was on the right path toward becoming a good doctor and a good surgeon.

***

The expected path for me following a preliminary residency was to then re-apply to a categorical residency in surgery or another specialty field in order to gain my board certification. However, I knew that I ultimately wanted to become a plastic surgeon. From my extensive library research during medical school, I knew that the minimum requirement for most plastic surgery fellowships was only three years of general surgery, even though the vast majority of students completed a five-year categorical program before applying to fellowships.

Many times in my academic and medical career, I had applied for long shots. The odds of even being in the position I was at that point—a medical doctor after arriving as a refugee a little over ten years earlier—was a one-in-a-million chance. I decided to apply for plastic surgery fellowships.

Once again, my unique background and an extraordinary amount of luck combined to bring me an unexpected result. Somehow, I was accepted to a plastic surgery fellowship at Tulane University in New Orleans. My scores on residency exams were mediocre, and I knew my letters of recommendation were not spectacular. The only reasons I can imagine for my acceptance are that the program director must have been impressed with my performance in the interview and my background as a refugee.

And so, in the summer of 1992, after just three years of preliminary residency in general surgery, I moved across the country to New Orleans to begin a fellowship in plastic surgery. This was the goal I had been working toward since the first week of medical school. I felt a deep sense of accomplishment, but also a profound trepidation. I knew that I would likely be younger and more inexperienced compared to my colleagues. It wouldn't help that I have always been small in stature and appeared younger than I really am.

The Tulane University plastic surgery fellowship was a two-year program, and they accepted just three plastic surgery fellows each year. When I arrived to meet my new colleagues, my fears were confirmed. Not only was I the youngest fellow by several years, I was *vastly* inexperienced compared to the other two. Both were white men who had each completed a full five-year categorical residency in general surgery. In addition, one had also been practicing as a general surgeon for several years following his residency. The other had completed seven years of general surgery, five years of clinical practice, and an additional two years of research and publishing. I felt so inadequate! I had only been out of medical school for three years. While these men had been starting their medical practice, I was still an ocean-tossed refugee, fighting for my daily survival.

In addition to being older and more experienced than me, my new colleagues were also *much* taller. One of the second-year fellows stood at 6' 2" and well over 250 pounds. He'd been drafted to play professional football after college but had turned the opportunity down in order to pursue medical school. If someone had taken a picture of my colleagues and me during those first few days, it would have looked like five grown white men standing next to a timid little Asian boy. The whole situation would have been comical if it wasn't so intimidating.

Despite these factors, I resolved to do what I had always done in my educational and medical career: I studied, worked hard, and tried to learn everything I could. I decided to see the other fellows as potential sources of knowledge and mentorship rather than intimidating competitors. Luckily, after seeing my enthusiasm to learn, they began to see me this way as well.

In fact, that ex-football player who towered over me and seemed so imposing turned out to be a generous mentor who took me under his wing during my first year at Tulane. He would joke about our size difference, saying he would beat up anyone who treated me poorly. But even though he was physically intimidating and much more experienced, he never made me feel small when answering my questions. He patiently and honestly shared much of the wisdom he'd gained from his experience, helping me learn along the way.

Moving to New Orleans was also a new cultural experience for me. The Tulane Medical Center was located in the heart of downtown, just a few blocks from the famous French Quarter. Of course, that meant that the annual Mardi Gras festival was impossible to ignore. I've never been drawn to large parties or crowds, but I had to see the famous Mardi Gras for myself. So, early one evening during the festival I walked through the French Quarter, taking in all the fantastic sights and sounds. Marching bands played in the streets. People wore outrageous, colorful costumes and masks, and everywhere I looked, people were dancing. It was exciting, but I felt out of place. I knew this was not my scene. And more than anything, I didn't want to jeopardize my fellowship by getting in any dangerous situation. I walked through the neighborhood but made sure to make my way back to my apartment near the hospital before nightfall when I knew the *real* party would begin.

I also learned to love Cajun cooking. The spicy seafood jambalaya and gumbo exposed me to new flavors I'd never experienced before. One thing I did not enjoy about New

PAUL LUU, MD

Orleans was the intense heat and humidity of the summers. Growing up in Vietnam, I was used to warm weather and humidity, but perhaps the mild climate of California had spoiled me. I found the sweltering conditions in New Orleans unbearable. During my two years there, I was more than happy to stay indoors most of the time, focused on learning everything I could from the more experienced medical professionals around me.

***

When I completed the plastic surgery fellowship in the summer of 1994, I could have then begun practicing medicine on my own or looked for a job with a larger practice. However, I still felt inadequate to go out into the "real world." At just 32 years old, I was still very young for a surgeon. And even though I now had five years of surgical training under my belt, I still felt inexperienced.

I had always enjoyed hand surgery, so I decided to apply for another fellowship that would allow me to pursue that specialty as well. Since I was already living in the south, I decided to apply for a program at University of Alabama in Birmingham, and I was accepted to a one-year fellowship there. It was time to move again for another year of medical training.

I only spent one year in Birmingham, and that was more than enough time for me! Compared to the vibrancy of New Orleans and Southern California, Birmingham felt like a boring city. But my time in the south was a good learning experience. With practice and dedication, I became a better surgeon and a better physician.

Still, throughout both fellowships, I always had a nagging sense of inadequacy. I knew I looked too young. I knew I spoke with an accent. Often, patients would give me quizzical looks, as if questioning whether I was really their doctor.

As the end of my hand fellowship approached, I knew that it was time for me to go out into the real world and begin my medical practice in earnest. I began thinking about where I might feel more comfortable and less like an inexperienced outsider. One surgeon I had met in New Orleans expressed interest in hiring me as a hand surgery specialist in his practice. He offered to pay me well, but something about this doctor rubbed me the wrong way. I could tell that he was interested in surgery primarily to make money rather than to help his patients, and that has never been my priority. I didn't want to insult him, so I made a polite excuse, saying I wanted to move back to the West Coast to be closer to my family. And in part, that was true. I had many fond memories of California where I'd gone to college and medical school, and I also thought I'd like to live somewhere with a large Vietnamese community, to serve and give back to other refugees and immigrants like myself.

***

I completed my hand fellowship in August of 1995. By then, I had made my mind up that I wanted to return to California. I packed up my small apartment and few belongings into a

U-Haul trailer, hitched it to my Jeep, and started the drive west.

At that time, one of my sisters who, like my parents and other siblings, had originally immigrated to Vancouver, was living in Seattle with her two young daughters. Her husband was away, studying to become a dentist in New Jersey. She urged me to come stay with her while I explored my options. She suggested I might even consider serving the large Vietnamese community in the Pacific Northwest.

This idea intrigued me. I thought back to that moment so many years ago as the pirates raided our boat. I had prayed to Phat Quan Âm, the Compassionate Buddha, for protection and promised to dedicate my life to helping others. From the beginning, my intention was to use my surgery skills to help all people. But opening a private practice catering to the Vietnamese immigrant community seemed like it could be a viable way to support myself financially while continuing to serve the wider population in the local hospitals. So, instead of driving straight to California, I turned north, and after many long days on the road, arrived in Seattle.

My sister welcomed me into her home where I met my young nieces, who were just babies. This was my first time living with a family member since leaving Vietnam. But just like when I visited my family in Vancouver, I found that we had little in common. My sister was just one year older than me, so we had grown up together, but we'd now been apart for so long. She was completely absorbed with raising her two girls. Meanwhile, my focus was on my fledgling career and trying to find a job. But I was grateful for my sister's hospitality and for her suggestion that I look for work so that I could help serve the Vietnamese population in Seattle.

Despite what my sister said, Seattle had never appealed to me. I knew its reputation as a gloomy, wet city. Compared to the sunshine and warm weather of Southern California, the choice seemed obvious. However, I wanted to show her my appreciation for letting me stay with her while I looked for jobs, so as soon as I arrived in Seattle, I contacted a few plastic surgery offices and a hand surgery group in the city. I let them know my background and training and inquired whether they were interested in hiring another surgeon.

To my surprise, the Seattle doctors were not welcoming at all. Every doctor or office I called told me they had no need for a new surgeon or they already had someone in mind, so I need not apply. It was as if they were insulted by the fact that a young surgeon would try to move into their territory and take away their patients. This was not my intention at all. I only wanted to establish myself in a community where I could make a difference and practice the skills I had spent so many years learning.

This brief experience left a bitter taste in my mouth and made me think even more that Seattle was not the place for me. Once again, I turned my attention to Southern California. I booked a plane ticket and flew down to Orange County where I knew there was a large Vietnamese immigrant community. Once there, I reached out to an older Vietnamese plastic surgeon named Dr. Tran Tien Sum who had been practicing there for many years. In contrast to the Seattle surgeons, this doctor was very kind to me. He agreed to meet with me and give me his thoughts on establishing myself in that community.

I met Dr. Tran at his office in Valencia, CA. He had a private practice there that specialized in both cosmetic and reconstructive surgery. To me, it seemed like he had somehow found a way to build a thriving practice in a competitive industry.

He welcomed me into his office and asked me about my plans as a surgeon. I gave him a brief history of my experience and medical training and told him that my priority was to practice somewhere with a large Vietnamese population. Listening to me, the doctor nodded along and acknowledged that he had similar priorities. In many ways, our philosophies aligned. I thought this was a good sign, and I began to wonder whether he might offer me a job as a partner in his practice.

However, after a few minutes of chatting, Dr. Tran said, "Paul, you seem like a dedicated surgeon, and I wish I could help you, but I'm not interested in hiring another surgeon at this time."

I felt a little disappointed, but not disheartened. I asked him what he thought of the prospect of setting up my own private practice.

"That is an option," he said. "But who would refer patients to you? You've only just finished your fellowship, and none of the other doctors here know you or your reputation."

I nodded.

"Do you have much money saved?" Dr. Tran asked. "Would you be able to afford the expense of opening your own practice?"

I nearly laughed. I had maybe $5,000 dollars in a savings account that I had managed to put away during my time as a resident. I thought about how I was living for free with my sister and her family in Seattle, unable to afford my own place. I looked around the nicely decorated office and thought about all the expenses of a building, exam rooms, and staff. The idea felt so far out of reach.

"No," I said finally, "I don't have much savings. I'm not sure how I would open an office like this one."

Dr. Tran smiled. "If you want my advice," he said, "I'd suggest finding another private practice to join or applying for a position at a multispecialty clinic. Build your reputation from there. I'm sure you'll find a good place to practice eventually."

I thanked him for his advice, we shook hands, and he showed me out of the building.

I stayed in Los Angeles for a few more days and made phone calls to various other plastic surgery and hand specialty clinics but didn't have any more luck. My prospects didn't seem any more promising in California than they had in Seattle.

On the plane ride back north, I turned the problem over and over in my head. It seemed to me like I had two options. I could continue to query other surgical practices, hoping that I would eventually find one willing to hire me, or I could take my chances and try to open a private practice somewhere despite other people's doubts.

The more I considered these options, the more I thought about Seattle. As far as I knew, there was no Vietnamese plastic surgeon who was focused on serving the large Vietnamese population in the city. Yes, the reception from other doctors in Seattle had been less than welcoming. But maybe I could establish a private practice and get enough work from the Vietnamese community to support myself while I built my reputation as a good surgeon in local hospitals.

I also thought about my family. In addition to my sister living in Seattle, my brother, parents, and other sisters were all living in Vancouver at that time. I had spent so much time away from my family by that point—pursuing my education—that I had begun to think of myself as independent from them. But I had to admit that having family close by once more felt nice, even if it was awkward or strained at times. My sister had already been so helpful and generous in letting me stay with her family in Seattle. Plus, my parents were aging, and if I could establish my medical practice somewhere close by, I would be more available to support them if they ever needed my help or had any medical problems.

During this time, another thought had also begun to creep into my mind. I hadn't been back to Vietnam since fleeing as a refugee in the spring of 1979. Part of me wanted to return to my home country to see if there was anything left of the world I'd known growing up. My medical education and early attempts at establishing a career had absorbed all my time and attention. I knew that if I didn't return now, I'd become so wrapped up in my career that it might be another decade or two before I made the trip. More than anything, I wanted to find some of the people who'd helped me early in my journey and thank them for their kindness.

By the time the plane touched down in Seattle, I had all but made up my mind. I resolved to use some of my meager savings to return to Vietnam, and when I returned, I would open a private medical practice in Seattle. I would build my reputation as a compassionate surgeon, working to fulfill the promise I had made all those years ago as a terrified refugee praying to Buddha for help. Meanwhile, I would support myself by catering to the Vietnamese population. I would be a force of compassion and care in the community, using the skills I had learned to help others.

13. Return to Vietnam and Establishing a Medical Practice

That September of 1995, I bought a plane ticket and flew from Seattle to Saigon. When I arrived, the first thing that struck me was how foreign I now felt in the country of my birth. I took a taxi to the center of Saigon and walked the streets I'd known as a child. On one level, everything was familiar to me. The shops, the sounds, the smells. They all came flooding back. But now I stood apart from them. My perspective had shifted completely. I'd become so Westernized and accustomed to my life in America.

The abject poverty of so many Vietnamese people struck me in a way that it never had before. The state of their clothes and homes shocked me. Of course, I had grown up in these conditions. As a refugee, I'd had nothing but the clothes on my back and what I could carry in a small suitcase. Now, more than sixteen years later, I felt uncomfortable moving through the city I'd fled. I saw poor and suffering people and wondered how I had managed to escape to a new life. I felt a desire to help each and every person I met, but I didn't know how.

One thing I could try to do was find one of the people who

had helped me. The primary person I wanted to find was Tran Quang Ai, the boy who had helped me hide the piece of fabric when my family's store was shut down. He'd acted so selflessly and affected my life in a way that had profound repercussions. I wanted to tell him in person how much I appreciated him. I remembered where he'd lived when we were boys, but after so many years, I had no idea if he'd still be there. I decided it was the best place to start.

I remembered the exact location of the junior high school we'd attended, and I remembered that Tran Quang Ai had lived nearby. I took a taxi to the neighborhood and surprised myself by how easily I was able to find his family's old home. I hesitated for a moment, feeling a sense of exhilaration at the prospect of seeing my old friend. I raised my hand and knocked on the door.

A man I did not recognize answered. "Can I help you?" he asked with a quizzical look.

"I'm looking for my friend, Tran Quang Ai," I said. "He lived here many years ago."

The man looked at me skeptically. I realized how strange I must have looked, a Vietnamese man wearing Western-style clothing suddenly arriving on his front step asking for someone he may have never heard of.

"The Tran family doesn't live here anymore," he said.

"But you knew them?" I asked, excitement rising in my voice. "Do you know where they've moved to?"

"I'm sorry," the man said, "I don't."

Disheartened, I turned away, and the man closed the door. But I couldn't give up my search that easily. While I was in the neighborhood, I decided to try the home of one of our mutual friends, Ta Hoang Dung, another of the five boys I'd been close to in junior high.

I walked a few streets over and found my other friend's old house. With any luck, I thought, someone there might remember where Tran Quang Ai and his family had moved. I knocked on the door.

A young man answered, another unfamiliar face.

"Hello," I said. "Does Ta Hoang Dung still live here?"

The man looked at me suspiciously. I explained who I was, an old friend back from America, and his face softened.

"That's my older brother," he said, "but he doesn't live here anymore. I can tell him you stopped by."

"Yes!" I said, excited to have found a lead. "Please do that. And ask him to come see me while I'm here."

I wrote down my uncle's address where I was staying, and the man assured me he would let his brother know.

Sure enough, the next morning, a familiar man arrived on a moped at my uncle's house. It was my old friend Ta Hoang Dung! The two of us spent a few minutes catching up before I asked him if he knew anything about Tran Quang Ai or where his family had moved. I told him I'd tried his old house but had been unable to track him down.

"Of course!" he said. "I have his phone number. We can call him together."

Excited, we rushed to my uncle's phone, and I waited while my friend dialed the number. After a few rings, there was an answer.

"Hello? Ai? You'll never guess who's here!"

He passed the phone to me, and I heard the distinct Huế accent I remembered from my childhood.

"Hello?"

Barely able to contain my excitement, I told Ai who I was and how happy it made me to hear his voice. Tran Quang Ai agreed to come visit me at my uncle's house that afternoon. I said goodbye to Ta Hoang Dung and waited.

Later that day, Ai did arrive, also by moped, and we greeted each other like the old friends we were. I recognized him immediately, but he looked much older than the last time I'd seen him. We were the same age, but he looked thin, and his skin had grown dark from the sun. Meanwhile, my time in the cafeterias and libraries of American universities had kept me looking well-fed and pale by comparison. We decided to walk to a nearby café where we could sit, have a drink, and catch up.

After Ai recovered from the initial shock of seeing me all these years later, he listened with amazement at my retelling of my journey to America and through the educational system. I thanked him profusely for the kindness he'd shown me so many years ago. He could not believe I remembered him and had tracked him down after so many years.

Unlike me, Ai had never left Vietnam. In fact, he told me with some embarrassment that his family had not been doing well. His wife had taken ill, and they'd gone broke trying to care for her.

My heart ached for my old friend. It seemed like just yesterday that we'd been classmates. Yet there I was, on the verge of beginning an exciting new career as a surgeon in the United States, and he was stuck in a cycle of poverty in Vietnam. I offered to give him some money to help his family, but he refused. I insisted, and finally he agreed to accept $100, which amounted to perhaps ten times his monthly income. I wished there was more I could do for him. At minimum, I hoped he could use the money to pay for his wife's medical treatment. I felt it was the least I could do for someone who had been such a good friend during such a difficult time for me and my family.

I wished my old friend well and hoped for his wife's speedy recovery. Already I was thinking about when I might be able to return to Vietnam to help my friend and so many others like him. But before I could do that, I had a career to establish back in the United States.

***

When I returned to Seattle, I was anxious to make some progress on my career. After my frustrating trip to California, the only path forward seemed to be opening a private practice. But coming to this decision did not make the journey ahead feel any more certain or clear. The main obstacle was that I didn't have any money to start a business. My meager savings were dwindling fast, and opening a medical office would require a significant investment. Luckily, before leaving the University of Alabama, I had been given some guidance in the area of medical businesses.

In the finance office at the hospital in Birmingham, there was a man named Mr. Roberts who gave me some advice. At the time, I still thought I might join a multi-specialty practice, but I also knew that starting my own business was a possibility. It felt prudent to have some understanding of the way it might work. So, I asked Mr. Roberts to meet with me to discuss financing options and the logistics of opening a medical practice. He kindly agreed and went through some examples of pro forma statements, profit and loss analyses, etc.

Using Mr. Roberts' templates, I put together a business plan for a new medical practice in Seattle. I was still nervous about striking out on my own, but I felt like if I could get some money to help establish myself, I might be able to succeed. Once the business plan was complete, I took it to US Bank and applied for a Small Business Administration loan.

The woman processing my application at the bank was extremely welcoming and kind. She knew that I was an immigrant and a new doctor, and she patiently went through my paperwork with me to ensure that everything was in place. With her help, I was approved for a $200,000 loan to start my business.

With my loan approved, the prospect of actually running my own medical practice now felt like an impending reality. I knew that I would have to be strategic and careful if I had any chance of success. So, I sat down at the kitchen table in my sister's apartment to think through and plan out my next steps. While looking for work in Seattle, I had done some research and discovered that I was the only Vietnamese plastic surgeon in the city. This put me in a unique position. As immigrants and refugees, I knew that many in my community might be uncomfortable approaching a white American doctor, especially for a cosmetic procedure. I believed there were enough Vietnamese immigrants in Seattle to support a private cosmetic surgery practice while I simultaneously worked to establish my reputation as a reconstructive and hand surgeon in the local hospitals.

It seemed like a reasonable plan. And so, in the fall of 1995, I applied for surgery privileges at the three main hospitals in Seattle: Swedish, Northwest, and Providence. Meanwhile, I started looking in earnest for a place to open the city's newest plastic surgery clinic.

***

In the mid-1990s, the Vietnamese community in Seattle was concentrated in the Rainer Valley neighborhood south of downtown. The area consisted of predominantly low-income housing and did not have the best reputation for being a safe or desirable neighborhood. Prostitutes regularly walked the streets at night, and the crime rate was high. Despite this, I knew that if I wanted to cater to the Vietnamese community, I needed to locate my office in the neighborhood where they lived.

One day, I drove down Rainier Avenue and noticed there was a vacant building on a corner lot. A sign in the window said, "for sale." I took down the number and called the real estate agent. She told me that the building was once a medical office, but that it had been closed for more than a year. The owner was looking to sell the property. It seemed like too good of an opportunity to turn down—not only a place to open my practice, but a chance to own the building as well. I arranged to meet the agent the following day.

The next morning, a pleasant woman named Jean Vel Dyke met me outside the closed medical office. I'm not sure what I was expecting, but I had not prepared for what confronted me when she opened the building's front door. It appeared that no human being had set foot inside during the entire year of vacancy. The space was dark and dusty. Spider webs hung down from the ceiling and surfaces. Miss Vel Dyke led me through the waiting room, offices and exam rooms, trying her best to highlight the potential, to help me imagine what the rooms could look like with a little cleaning and some fresh paint.

In addition to being neglected, the space was also larger than it looked from the outside, larger than I really needed at the time. In total, it was just under 3000 square feet, with several exam and procedure rooms. I was nervous to take on such a project, but I figured that if the price was reasonable, I might be able to make it work.

After we finished the tour of the building, I asked Miss Vel Dyke about the price.

"The seller is asking $250,000," she said.

My heart sank. My small business loan application had been approved for a maximum of $200,000, and that was supposed to be for business startup expenses, not to purchase a building. I decided to be honest with the real estate agent, to see if there were any other options.

"That's more than I can afford," I said. "But the location is perfect for what I'm hoping to do."

I explained to her my plan for a plastic surgery practice catering to the Vietnamese community. Miss Vel Dyke listened to my plan with interest. Somehow, she was impressed with my plan, and she trusted me.

"I'll tell you what," she said. "I think the owner might be willing to come down to $230,000. If you can put up $50,000 in cash, I can help you finance the rest. You can pay the building off over the next few years."

I was floored! Once again here was a total stranger going out of their way to help me along my journey. Of course, Miss Vel Dyke wanted to sell the building for her client. But she was taking on a big risk in helping me—a new doctor with no prior business experience—finance the purchase of a building.

I thanked Miss Vel Dyke profusely and then drove straight to US Bank to see if I could make the transaction happen. The loan officer at the bank acted hesitant at first. After all, the small business loan was not really supposed to be used to purchase real estate. But after I explained my plan, the woman agreed that I could use $50,000 of my $200,000 loan as a down payment.

"Just don't mention it too loudly," she told me with a smile as we were signing the final paperwork.

And just like that, I was the proud owner of a medical office building—albeit a rundown one—in the Rainier Valley neighborhood of Seattle.

***

The building at the corner of Rainier Avenue and Lucille Street also became my home. After finalizing the purchase of the building, I moved my few belongings from my sister's apartment into one of the exam rooms, which became my bedroom. One of the bathrooms included a shower as well, so it was a relatively comfortable place to stay.

For the next few weeks, I used every spare moment to get my new building ready for opening. I cleaned every inch of the space, wiping the layers of dust off surfaces and knocking the cobwebs out of corners. I hired some Vietnamese handymen from the neighborhood to help me paint and make minor repairs to the building.

Meanwhile, I also started working as a surgeon at the local hospitals. As a new doctor in town, I did not have relationships with other practitioners who could refer patients to me, but I managed to get on the call schedule for the emergency rooms. So, while working on the office building, if the hospital called me, I would jump in my car and drive to the emergency room at Swedish, Northwest, or Providence hospitals.

I also accepted calls late at night or early in the morning. Once, I was awakened after midnight by a phone call. The emergency room had a patient with a minor laceration to his face. It was the kind of procedure that many surgeons would just leave until the morning. But I told the nurse I would be there as soon as possible. I threw on my clothes and drove the 20 minutes from my new office building to the hospital. When I arrived and went in to see the patient, I overheard him asking the ER nurse whether I was really his surgeon. She assured him that I was, but the man said I looked too young to be a doctor. I ignored the comment and gave him the same attention and treatment I gave all my patients. I completed the surgery and drove back to my office as the sun was rising, turning Mt. Rainier pink in the distance as I turned onto Rainier Avenue.

Experiences like this left me exhausted and frustrated, but I did my best not to let them affect me. I wanted to establish a reputation as a reliable and adept surgeon, so I never turned down a call. I took every case, no matter how minor or if it meant interrupting a renovation project.

Despite my best efforts, those first few months of surgery at the hospitals did not always go smoothly. I was a new face at the hospital, so many patients—and even some staff—expressed skepticism about my skills. It didn't help that I looked so young compared to my colleagues and that I preferred to dress casually—usually wearing a clean polo shirt and slacks rather than a suit and tie or a white coat.

Through some combination of my youth, my casual style, and my accent, many patients—whether they expressed it verbally or with body language—did not trust me.

Once, I had a surgery scheduled at Providence Hospital on Cherry Hill in Seattle. I was brand-new and hadn't yet learned my way around the facility. After parking my car in the garage, I went into the building and asked at the front desk for them to point me toward the operating room. Instead of showing me the correct way, the old lady volunteering at the desk pointed me toward the cafeteria.

"No," I explained. "I'm a surgeon. I need to go to the operating room."

The woman looked straight at me for a moment and then asked, "Are you sure? You look too young to be a surgeon."

Annoyed as I was, I forced a smile. "Yes, I'm sure," I said, showing her my hospital ID.

Without seeming the least bit embarrassed at her mistake, the woman pointed me toward the elevator to the operating room.

Episodes like this could have discouraged me or made me doubt myself. But I did my best not to let them affect me. I marched on, worked hard, and let my skills in surgery and my compassionate bedside manner speak for themselves.

***

In addition to being on call for emergency surgeries, I also wanted to be placed on the call schedule for hand surgery at one or more of the hospitals. I had completed a hand and microsurgery fellowship at the University of Alabama. I wanted to use these skills and increase my caseload so that I could get myself established in Seattle's medical community.

Around the same time I moved to Seattle, two other young plastic surgeons also arrived. Like me, they were doing their best to work into existing schedules and build their practices. One of them had also completed a hand surgery fellowship. Together, the three of us approached the older surgeons who controlled the call schedule for hand surgeries at Northwest Hospital.

They answered that the schedule was made each calendar year, and that it was impossible to add someone mid-year. That seemed reasonable. It was late fall by this time, so we asked to be added to the new call schedule at the beginning of the next year. Perhaps I was naive to expect they would accommodate our request.

As the new year approached, the hand surgeons released their new call schedule. Surprise, surprise—the young surgeons were not added to the list. It was unbelievable! I couldn't understand how these older surgeons could be so unwilling to help a couple of young doctors get on their feet. One of the other new hand surgeons was even more furious. He threatened to bring legal action against the doctors if they did not agree to add us to the call schedule. To me, this seemed like an extreme measure, but I waited to see what their response would be.

In the end, the threat of a lawsuit was enough to make the older hand surgeons agree to let us on the schedule. But when they showed us the revised schedule, the other new surgeon and I were slated to split half of a regular call schedule. They had technically given us what we asked for, but at the absolute bare minimum. The whole ordeal left a bad taste in my mouth, but I was not interested in fighting the older surgeons any further. I didn't want to make enemies in my new community. As I always had, I tried not to let the actions of others affect me. I focused my energy on my medical practice and doing the best for my patients.

***

During those first few months in Seattle, I grew to love what I did for a living. Each time I approached a new case—whether a small reconstruction or a large facial fracture—I treated every patient with care from beginning to end. Being a good surgeon meant more to me than deftly cutting and sewing. From the moment I first met the patient in an exam room or emergency department to the moment they were discharged from the hospital, I treated them holistically. I did my best to consider not only their current condition but their previous medical history, their social situation, and their potential fears or anxiety.

My biggest allies in this work were the nurses at each hospital. In many instances, surgeons come in for a quick procedure and may not see a patient again for several days or weeks. But the nursing staff are there every day, taking care of patients' minute-by-minute needs. Unlike some doctors who see themselves as above the nurses, I always treated them as colleagues, professionals who had valuable knowledge and experience to share.

I grew particularly fond of the nursing staff at Northwest Hospital. They appreciated my approach and willingness to listen to their opinions and concerns before deciding on a course of treatment. In addition, I think they also respected that I took on all the cases that other surgeons didn't want to do. For example, at Northwest Hospital, I sometimes treated patients suffering from pressure sores due to paralysis—either paraplegics or tetraplegics. If the sores went long enough without attention or treatment, a deep wound would develop, sometimes deep enough to expose bone. In these cases, soft tissue reconstruction was necessary to repair the damage. Difficult surgeries like these were unpleasant and not lucrative for a plastic surgeon because many patients were on Medicaid or lacked insurance coverage. Not many plastic surgeons wanted to do them, but I always volunteered. In my view, each patient deserved the best care we could give them, regardless of their condition or financial situation.

In this way, my reputation started to grow at the local hospitals in Seattle. I seemed to be a good fit at Northwest Hospital. More and more, other doctors referred their patients to me until the majority of my reconstructive practice ended up at Northwest.

Meanwhile, I had finally opened the doors on my private practice. As I had planned, people in the Vietnamese community of south Seattle began coming to me, primarily for cosmetic procedures. Even though I was new to the area and looked young, people in this community trusted me. I spoke their language and could relate to many of their stories about leaving home as refugees. Many also believed that since I had studied medicine in the West, rather than in Vietnam, I must have adequate training and skills.

And so, I carried along with these two parallel tracks—reconstructive and occasional hand surgery at the hospitals and cosmetic surgery in my private practice. The more time I spent working as a doctor, the more I enjoyed it. If for some reason I had to go a few days or a week without seeing my patients, I felt like something was missing. Even now, when I go on vacation, I always try to find a local hospital to visit. Just walking through the halls makes me feel happy and at home.

I get the same feeling when I visit a university campus. I like to go to the student union buildings and watch all the energetic students coming and going. They're so full of youthful energy and potential. It reminds me of my own college experience. Since coming to the United States, these two environments have been so formative to my life. A university helped me survive and thrive in my young adulthood, to adapt to my new country. And the medical field has given me purpose and shown me my life's work.

When some people think about plastic surgery, they imagine wealthy doctors performing facelifts and breast augmentations for movie stars. But I never wanted to become that kind of plastic surgeon. Making a bunch of money was not important to me. I only wanted to support myself and do the best for my patients. If I stuck to that mission, I felt confident that enough money would come along. For that reason, I have always made it my practice to do surgery on any patient who needs the procedure, regardless of their ability to pay. If someone does not have insurance but is in pain or suffering, how could I not help them?

At times, however, my love of medicine and drive to do the best for every patient can be a curse as well as a blessing. Not every surgery has a perfect outcome. That is a fact of the imperfect world we live in. But whenever something doesn't go the way I hope—even a simple post-surgery infection—I end up replaying every detail over and over in my mind. I'll go home at the end of the day, obsessing over the patient's chart, wondering what I missed and what I could have done differently. I suppose I'm a perfectionist. But I hope it leads me toward more compassionate and competent care for my patients.

Over the next few months and years, my medical practice

slowly grew and began to thrive. After two years, I was able to buy my own home and finally move out of the room I had converted to a living space in the back of the office. I gradually built a solid reputation among the staff and doctors at Seattle's hospitals while also cultivating trust and a steady flow of patients to my private practice in the Vietnamese community. Without these dual tracks, it's unlikely that I would have been able to survive as a doctor in Seattle.

My medical career has been like many aspects of my journey, a combination of hard work, luck, and help from kind people around me. Through this combination, I have been fortunate enough to do what I truly love for more than two decades. But as satisfied as I felt in my professional life, I began to realize that something was missing. I kept thinking back to that prayer I had made as a terrified refugee, standing on the deck of a boat overrun by pirates, looking down into the foreboding water as a shark circled our hull. Had I really fulfilled the promise I made that day to use my skills to help those who were most in need? I knew that I could never feel fully satisfied with my life until I followed through on that commitment.

14. Fulfilling a Promise

As soon as I began to feel somewhat comfortable and established in my career as a surgeon in Seattle, I began looking for ways that I could volunteer or apply my skills to help the less fortunate. I started researching various nonprofit organizations in Seattle that might be a good fit. Of course, there were many doing vital work in the community, but none stood out to me as something I'd like to devote my time toward. It also occurred to me to look in Vietnam, my home country. I knew that I'd been extremely lucky to escape as a refugee in the way I had and that many others had not been as fortunate.

In the fall of 2007, while I was beginning this process, I happened to attend a plastic surgery seminar in Palm Springs, California. During one of the sessions, I was surprised to see Dr. Tran Tien Sum, the same doctor I'd met with in Southern California when considering where I should open my medical practice. We chatted for a while, catching up on everything that had transpired in the years since. He seemed genuinely glad to hear that I had managed to establish a successful office in Seattle.

We ended up spending more time together during the seminar, and one day, he gave me and another colleague a ride back to our hotel after a day of meetings and presentations. I was sitting in the back seat, looking out the window when I casually mentioned my interest in someday volunteering in Vietnam.

"You should come with me," he said. "Last year, I went back to Vietnam to do free surgery and teach at a local hospital."

The conversation happened in such an impromptu way that I was taken aback. I'd been doing so much research and planning, and here an opportunity to volunteer had fallen straight into my lap.

It turned out that prior to coming to the United States, Dr. Tran had been a professor of anatomy at a university in the city of Huế, Vietnam. He'd been introduced to the field of plastic surgery by some internationally renowned physicians visiting Saigon, including Dr. Arthur Barsky and Dr. Lester Silver, who later went on to become Chief of Plastic Surgery at Mt. Sinai Medical Center in New York. After fleeing the communist regime in 1975, Dr. Tran was accepted to a plastic surgery fellowship at Mt. Sinai where he trained with Dr. Silver. He then opened his private practice in Southern California where I had first met him as a young doctor.

Now that Dr. Tran was approaching his retirement, he wanted to reconnect with the Huế School of Medicine to teach and give back to the community he had come from. And he was looking for more doctors to join him.

I agreed to join Dr. Tran on an upcoming trip to Vietnam for two reasons. First, I remembered that during my plastic surgery fellowship at Tulane University, I'd met a brilliant Vietnamese orthopedic surgeon named Dr. Pham Dinh Nhat. He'd come to the United States on a traveling fellowship to learn about the field of plastic surgery, which at the time was not well-established in my home country. I'd stayed in touch with Dr. Pham after he returned to Vietnam, and I remembered that he was now practicing in the city of Huế. In fact, I later learned that he was now the chief of the orthopedic department at the Huế Central Hospital. I knew that a volunteer trip to Huế would allow me the chance to reconnect with Dr. Pham.

But more importantly, the trip offered me the chance to return to the country of my birth and give back to my countrymen who had not been afforded the chances I had. Perhaps it was one way that I could begin to fulfill the promise I made all those years ago to the Compassionate Buddha.

I returned to Seattle after the seminar but continued to stay in touch with Dr. Tran. And a few short months later, in the spring of 2008, I made my first of many annual volunteer trips to Vietnam.

***

After so many years of training and practice as a physician in the United States, I was shocked by the conditions I encountered during that first visit to the Huế School of Medicine. The young surgeons and residents at the hospital were eager to learn and doing the best they could with limited resources, but some of their equipment and conditions were truly appalling. The surgical instruments were the same as those used prior to the war in the 1960s and '70s. To me, it seemed like using a butcher knife to cut and a harpoon to sew!

I truly grew to admire the local surgeons' skill and their ability to perform complex surgeries with such crude equipment. However, I also discovered that most of the young surgeons lacked a basic understanding of medicine and post-surgical care. They had learned the mechanics of surgery from observing their instructors without learning the theory or background behind each surgical maneuver or procedure. This was not due to a lack of diligence or intelligence but simply a lack of access to Western textbooks and medical journals.

Now, more than a decade later, the internet has vastly improved access to medical information. And Vietnam's more stable economy has allowed hospitals to afford more modern equipment and supplies. However, many of the "bad habits" I observed during my first visit to Huế have remained. Bedside manner and patient communication, for example, are still severely lacking. Vietnamese doctors are often shocked to see me sitting at a patient's bedside, holding their hand, and talking with them about their lives—personal things that are not related to their medical care. This is far from the norm in Vietnamese culture. Often, doctors don't even sufficiently explain procedures or post-operative care, which can result in infections or other complications. There also continues to be unsafe attitudes toward sterilization and cleanliness protocols.

Many operating rooms are dirty, and people move in and out of them during procedures like it's an open marketplace.

These cultural attitudes and practices are much more difficult to change than equipment or medical knowledge. That is the real challenge and work during my volunteer trips to Vietnam.

***

Following that first trip to Vietnam, Dr. Tran formed the Tran Tien Foundation which focuses on funding pro bono surgery and promoting the field of plastic surgery in Huế. Since 2008, I have returned each spring with Dr. Tran and a group of volunteer doctors from the United States. Due to the COVID-19 pandemic, we were unable to travel to Vietnam from 2020 to 2022, but we hope to resume our volunteer trips as soon as we're able.

We typically arrive on a Sunday and examine patients from 8 a.m. to 5 p.m. at the two largest hospitals in Huế. Suitable patients are then selected for surgery and scheduled for the coming week. Generally, these patients need some kind of reconstructive surgery, resulting from cleft palates, burns, hand injuries, trauma, cancer or congenital deformities.

Monday through Friday, all the visiting surgeons perform procedures beginning at 8 a.m. and sometimes lasting late into the evening. Always, we work alongside the local surgeons or residents, helping them develop their technique and medical best practices. Usually, we're able to perform 50 to 75 free surgeries during the week. On Saturday, we present a full day of lectures and seminars on various topics before flying home.

This is rewarding work for me. Each patient I'm able to help, and each young surgeon or resident I can mentor, feels like a victory. Yet every year, I spend just this single week volunteering in Vietnam. It feels like such a short time. It's hard to know whether I'm making any lasting impact. Perhaps this feeling goes back to my tendency to be a perfectionist. In one week, I can help a few individual patients and maybe consult with a few local surgeons on difficult cases. But there is so much need and so few problems that can truly be "solved" in just one week.

To me, medicine is more than just mastering the knowledge and skills necessary to treat patients. In order to be a good doctor, you also have to develop a certain respect for the practice and a level of empathy that allows you to treat each patient with compassion. I believe anyone can master the technical side of surgery. You could take any reasonably competent lay person and teach them to do surgery—much the way you might train a car mechanic. But a human being is not a machine. And becoming a good surgeon is about more than learning to cut and sew. To me, it also means taking care of an entire patient, physically and emotionally, from beginning to end.

I often express this philosophy to my Vietnamese colleagues. But this is by far the most difficult lesson. It cannot be learned in one week. Medicine is a practice, something that must be developed and improved upon throughout the course of an entire career. You have to be willing to be a continual student of the art and science of medicine. In fact, often when people ask my profession, I will tell them I am a student. It's true—I am always striving to learn more about my vocation.

So, this is my challenge each time I return to Vietnam. I can see every year the local surgeons' technical skills improving, but the way they approach their patients largely remains the same. Pre- and post-operative care, bedside manner, interactions between doctors and nursing staff—the intangible skills are the most difficult to master. Still, I believe I can make a difference. I know from personal experience that with hard work and diligence, any situation can be gradually improved. That is why I continue to return to Vietnam each year. The doctors and staff at the hospitals always tell me they are grateful for my time, but I wish I had more to give.

Each time I return to Vietnam, I also look for my friend Tran Quang Ai. I've been unable to reconnect with him since that first visit in 1995. Every year, I ask neighbors and mutual friends, but no one seems to know what has become of him. More recently, I've searched for him on Facebook and online but have been unable to find him. After so many years, I still feel like there is more I could do to help lift him and his family out of poverty. But the world is round, and I believe someday I will see my old friend again.

Perhaps when I retire from full-time practice in Seattle, I will be able to devote more of my time and energy to volunteer work. Already, my colleagues in Vietnam have invited me to come teach full-time. Perhaps I will find an orphanage in Vietnam where I can work with local children while also teaching and performing surgery at the hospital.

But other colleagues have extended offers as well. One doctor, who I got to know during my residency at Harbor-UCLA Medical Center, has worked for hospitals throughout the developing world. He is a family medicine physician named Dr. William Clemmer. During his career, he has spent time at a Baptist hospital in the Congo and now works with the Bill and Melinda Gates Foundation and the UN, helping to establish medical systems in the refugee camps of South Sudan.

I've asked him about working with refugees in Africa in some capacity, but he has told me frankly, "Paul, right now I don't have much use for a surgeon like you because we don't have the infrastructure for surgery in the refugee camps."

However, when he finishes his current commitment, he plans to return to the Congo where he has offered me a standing invitation to visit and help. So, I plan to spend some time in Africa once I retire as well.

In the meantime, I still feel a commitment to my patients in Seattle. In recent years, I have narrowed the scope of my reconstructive practice to focus on wound care at the hospital now known as UW Medicine–Northwest Campus. These are often difficult cases that other surgeons are reluctant to take on—very old or paralyzed patients with pressure sores or other injuries. There is no "fun" or "glory" in treating these patients. Many plastic surgeons would rather dedicate their time toward breast reconstructions or cosmetic surgery, but I always treat them. And through some combination of luck, aptitude, and support from the nursing staff, I generally have good results.

But each time I see one of these patients, I take on some of their suffering. Yes, I treat them as a surgeon, but the connection I feel goes much deeper than that. I feel as if they are a part of me or a member of my family. To see a fellow human being in such pain—to be totally paralyzed and dependent on others for every daily activity—eats away at me. I want to alleviate their suffering but also somehow share their burden.

I'm now 60 years old, and I believe I still have another 15-20 productive years of life left. I am embarking upon a new chapter, one in which I hope to find a way to take care of the needy, handicapped, or less fortunate. All those years ago, as a frightened refugee clutching a water jug as a last hope of survival while pirates searched our boat, I made a promise to the Compassionate Buddha. If I lived through the ordeal, I pledged to use my skills and energy to help those in the world who are needy. I survived. And I don't believe I've yet fulfilled that promise. That is the goal toward which I intend to dedicate the remainder of my life.

I want to do this in order to find a sense of peace, but also to pass forward the compassion that was shown to me by so many people along my journey. So many friends and strangers went out of their way to help me survive and achieve my goal of becoming a surgeon. They helped me reach the point where I can practice the craft I truly love. It is for them that I work so hard. And it is out of gratitude toward them that I share this story. Thank you to everyone who showed me kindness as a refugee. Thank you to the nursing and medical staff who mentored and nurtured me. And of course, thank you to my family—especially my parents—who taught me how to be compassionate toward others and set me upon the path to the man I have become.

About the Author

Dr. Paul Luu was born in Vietnam and left his home country in 1979 at the age of sixteen. Through hard work, an unshakable sense of hope, lots of luck, and help from caring individuals and mentors, Paul managed to earn a GED, attend college at University of the Pacific, and then medical school at UCLA. After years of competitive medical internships and fellowships, Paul became a plastic surgeon specializing in reconstructive and hand surgery. He currently owns and operates a private medical practice in Seattle's Rainier Valley and makes frequent trips back to Vietnam to volunteer his medical services.